Cover design by Creativewithryan.com

ISBN: 978-1-3999-6680-1

www.afmarseh.com
@AfMarseh

TUMOROUS
HESTICLES

Just Say Cancer

BY

AF MARSEH

To respect the privacy of the people mentioned in this book, some names have been altered. Despite these changes, approximately 93% of this book remains entirely factual.

Contents

Introduction

Hello mate,

I'm going to call you mate for now as we've only just met, but by the end of this book, we'll have a connection and who knows maybe even become friends.

I hear you've booked onto your next adventure: cancer. Damn!

It's not the most exciting adventure you'll ever have. It's not climbing a mountain, it's not snorkelling with turtles and it's not Vegas. But it's an adventure nonetheless. It'll teach you a few life lessons and you'll be living the dream again soon enough.

Firstly, I'm not going to dress it up or mince my words as we don't have time to waste and life's too short. Cancer is shit. We all know it's shit... BUT it's manageable with the right preparation, support network and mindset.

This will probably be a complete whirlwind for you and your family. Sometimes the cancer and the treatment are the easy part. People just start crying all the time and you can feel like the burden. Sometimes you'll start crying yourself. Crying in front of people, crying on your own and sometimes just crying at random shit like a moving Britain's Got Talent audition. It's all fine. You cry when you want to cry, and if there are times you're not crying, and you feel weirdly guilty about it, that's fine too. There is no rule book. You've had the shit news of being welcomed to the cancer club. So, strap in and read when you want to read, sleep when you want to sleep and definitely laugh when you want to laugh.

This will be one of the most surreal experiences you'll ever have. You'll have so many questions rushing through your mind that you won't have time to take in all of the answers. Some questions might need clinical information which require scans and blood tests. Some questions might just be, 'How much will it hurt?'

One fellow cancer brother (yes, I have cancer friends now) phoned me up for the first time when he was diagnosed. 'It's not actually that bad, is it?' he asked sheepishly.

I had to be honest with him. 'Mate this is fucking horrible…but you can beat it.'

What you also have to prepare yourself for is people asking YOU questions. Questions that become repetitive, mundane and feel senseless. People will ask you where you were when you found a lump and how you're feeling during chemotherapy, which seem like pretty pointless questions to ask as the treatment goes on. But it's one of the many, many 'meaningless' and repetitive questions that people will continue to ask. You're going to be the talk of the town now and everyone wants to know. You're the star of the show. Of course, the people that ask these questions aren't trying to annoy you, frustrate you or quiz you. They're trying to show you that they care and have an interest. If you're one of the people who have asked these questions, don't worry. It's not that bad. Way better than awkward silences, that's for sure.

I took quite a public approach to sharing my cancer journey but I'm quite the social media whore anyway.

That's just me! Would I do it all the same way if it happened again? Probably not, but I can tell you what helped and what I could have done better.

I'm hoping this book will support cancer victims and sufferers along their journey, but it will also give non-victims an insight into what goes on during a cancer process. Even the word 'victim' sounds pretty dramatic doesn't it? At stages you will be a victim. But that includes the mums, dads, siblings, friends and partners of a cancer patient. It's not just the person going through the treatment who is suffering through these journeys. Sometimes the inability to help or take away the pain can cause suffering to your support network too.

In my experience, I found the people that talk most 'honestly' about cancer are the ones who have been through it themselves. I'll be 100% honest and sometimes honest is blunt, sometimes honest is sad, and sometimes honest is just funny. You'll have people in your life that make cancer seem 'not so bad' because they want you to feel comfortable, which is great. We definitely need these people in our lives. Friends will tell you that you look better than they thought you would, and then you'll also have people who'll refuse to even say the word cancer and use phrases like 'the big C' or 'he's sick' – just like my dad chose to. And that's fine too.

You'll hear the c-word more times than ever before. No, not that c-word. You'll start to notice every cancer advert on the television and bus stops with 'beat cancer' advertising boards. You'll hear of more people being diagnosed or even dying.

So, let's get used to that word. Cancer. It's just a word, after all, isn't it?

Maybe not.

It carries a greater meaning this time because we know people who've suffered with it. It's taken our loved ones from us and now poses a threat to you or someone you know. But when you beat this, it won't define you and you'll grow and move on from it and become .... (insert name here) once again.

Remember, you got this!

Greetings

My name's Af. It's short for Afsheen Panjalizadeh-Marseh Junior the fifth, so yeah, Af is perfectly fine. I'm thirty-five years old and six years into remission. I was diagnosed when I was twenty-nine and just a regular lad with a love of sports, socialising over a beer, and trying to find my future wife. I love travelling, adventures and challenges. I've driven a Rickshaw 2,000 miles across the length of India for charity. I've run four marathons whilst never claiming to be a runner. I've cycled from London to Paris in three days and don't own a bike. I've climbed a few mountains. I've even been on *The Chase* game show and of course went for the higher offer of £36,000, just to make my friends laugh at home, ultimately crashing out in a blaze of glory on national TV. The presenter Bradley Walsh shook my hand as I walked off and said, 'Af, you may have lost, but you've brought so much sunshine to everyone's lives.'

Wow, thanks Bradley – I can use that quote in a book one day!

I think this pretty much sums up my life so far. Aiming high and just losing but spreading sunshine as I go.

I guess someone or something has led you here because you've recently been diagnosed. You don't know what to expect and you're in a chemotherapy chair or bed, bored out of your mind. Or you might be a friend or relative of a sufferer and this book will show you what's going through a young man's mind and how you might help them during this challenge. This is going to be a team effort. Champions don't win without their support networks. Usain Bolt doesn't just run the fastest one hundred metres without the support of his family, coaches and fans. So, come on sisters, brothers, mothers and lovers – this is a team challenge! That's all it is – and we all love a challenge.

When I was first diagnosed, I received gifts, flowers and cards all with well wishes and love. One card was from my previous job, signed by ex-colleagues and my former boss. My boss wrote in it: *Just another challenge*. That was it – no good luck, no best wishes, no kisses. It made me laugh but that was him; he was crazy in terms of challenges and not displaying much emotion. He reminded me of my dad.

My boss's leadership style wasn't for everyone because no matter how big my achievement was, it could've always been better. Just like my dad. I'm sure my ex-boss and my dad are proud of the achievements that I've made, but both rarely said it out loud. My ex-boss competed in his first Ironman race at 50 years old, pushed me up the 3 peaks challenge on 3 separate occasions and once made me dig a snow hole in the Scottish Highlands and sleep in it for the night. It felt like a form of workplace bullying, but he always referred to it as character building. I was used to it from years of tough love from Dad.

If there are two people who might not open up about their feelings as much then it's my boss who grew up in the east end of London in the 70s, and my dad who grew up in Iran during the 60s. Both had conquered challenges throughout life so I guess my boss thought cancer would be just another challenge and require the same old attributes of perseverance, battling on and never giving up.

There's no other place to start on this adventure than when you first noticed something was wrong. It doesn't actually happen as theatrically as it does on the television, does it? It's not a one-off trip to the doctors and they tell you the news in dramatic fashion and everyone drops to their knees in tears. It takes a number of 'it could be, but it's probably not' appointments that happen one after the other. By the time you're told its cancer, it's already been suggested to you so many times that in a way you've already braced for it.

I'm going to talk you through this book and hopefully you can dip in and out of it when you feel strong enough. You can read ahead if you want to brace yourself for the next chapters of the journey such as losing your hair or how sick you'll feel. Equally, you can just live the challenge yourself and then come back and read parts of this book and say to yourself, 'Yeah, that's how I felt.' Just so you know you're not going through it alone. The first thing my friend Julian said when he welcomed me to Cancer Club was, 'The first rule of Cancer Club is it's ok to talk about cancer. The second rule of Cancer Club is it's ok to talk about cancer.'

Post cancer, I've been contacted by lots of people asking me to talk to their friends who've recently been diagnosed. They all started as total strangers, but I was someone to lean on throughout their journeys, just like my friend Julian was for me.

After the first year of the all-clear I was just focussing on finding myself again. The emotional rollercoaster and chemotherapy had drained my body and mind, and this might happen to you as well.

Gulp! Don't be anxious just yet – we're all different.

During the second year of remission, I wanted to be done with cancer altogether. I didn't want to talk about it anymore, didn't want to associate with it and didn't want it to define me. Now, beyond my fifth year, I figure I can support, motivate and inspire people around the world with this challenge.

Five years into remission, a lot has changed. Not just for me but for everyone who was around me during my journey. We were all suffering at some point: Mum, Dad, my sister, brother, grandparents and friends. It was a nightmare and it felt like it was all my fault. Everyone was trying to bring me up from the slums of despair, but all I was doing was bringing them down. Without even trying.

Cancer teaches so many life lessons to everyone involved so I've decided to start each chapter with a life lesson and a cancer lesson that you may be able to relate to. I've also included a song choice for each chapter as sometimes music is the answer and I've tried to make each song relate to your story at that specific time.

This is one man's cancer story. Cancer for men is similar to man flu, just a whole lot worse. Everyone knows man flu is worse than normal flu and man cancer is even tougher than that. Men don't talk about emotions like women tend to, we don't do Race for Life and wear pink in solidarity, our friends don't buy us flowers and comment on our Facebook photos saying, 'You look beautiful, hun.'

We drink beer, we watch sports, and we ignore it.

Because we're men and we're hard.

Aren't we?

1.   Where Were You?

Life Lesson: Men are useless.
Cancer Lesson: Just another challenge.
Song Choice: *Life is Live* – Opus

I was laying on the concrete floor holding my balls, with tears streaming down my face. It was the most pain I'd ever felt in my life. To add insult to injury, everyone in the entire school's playground was looking at me. Shaun Groves, my best friend in primary school, had just booted me in the testicles like he was trying to kick them back into my stomach. It felt like he'd succeeded.

During the school lunch break, we'd arranged a football penalty shoot-out. Whoever won would take one of the Spice Girls on an imaginary date. We were ten years old. Shaun had missed his final penalty and I slotted mine in the bottom corner to win the love of Emma Bunton; Baby Spice. As I ran around Shaun over-celebrating and windmilling my arms, he booted me between the legs, sending me into a heap on the floor.

At the end of the school day, Shaun's mum marched him up to me at the school gates and made him apologise. We remained great friends, but boy, was his love for Baby Spice not to be messed with.

Maybe this provoked attack on my balls was the start of the germ cell mutation to give me cancer nineteen years later. Probably not.

Maybe my cancer actually started fourteen years later when I returned from a trip to Sweden with a testicle

11

looking like a large coconut. I'd signed up to take part in the Viking Run, an eighty-kilometre ice skating challenge across frozen lakes, finishing in Stockholm. After six months of training, which consisted of rollerblading to my work in Essex and ice skating at Chelmsford Ice Rink on the weekends, the race was cancelled. They'd had a warm week in Sweden and the ice was too dangerous to skate on. We would have literally been skating on thin ice. Instead, I spent three nights partying in Stockholm and came back to the UK with a serious case of the mumps. My glands had swollen up to make my neck disappear and one bollock had swollen to the size of a grapefruit. I was hospitalised for two weeks, signed off work for six weeks, and was very sick. Maybe this is how I got cancer?

Maybe it was wearing pants that were too tight, taking too many hot baths, being on my mobile phone too much and receiving radio-active waves, or maybe my balls didn't drop early enough as a child.

The thing is, no one ever asks, 'How did you get cancer?' They just ask how did you find it and where were you?

Reflection is a positive process, so before we jump into the cancer shenanigans, let's look at where *you* were in your life when it all started. It might even be where you are in life right now. Maybe your cancer journey started when you were just floating along in life. Maybe you were riding high or even struggling at rock bottom when it all happened. Let's be honest, there's never a good time to be diagnosed with cancer.

I want you to think about what you have around you that could make this challenge more manageable.

What have you got right now in your version of Maslow's hierarchy of needs? House? Job? Partner? Money? Well, I had nothing, but at the same time, I had everything! Happiness, freedom and chasing my dreams. I was shooting for the top of my metaphorical mountain. I was at a stage where I had rolled the dice and taken a gamble in life. At first, my lucky dice were winning with every roll but sooner rather than later, the dice didn't just fail me, they rolled off the table and got crushed into a thousand pieces resulting in surgery and chemotherapy. Whoever came up with 'roll the dice and take a leap of faith' was very wrong this time. In a way…

I love enticing my mates into a night out on the town for 'just a couple of beers' and then rolling in at 4am not knowing why I got the extra chilli sauce on my kebab and why the dog is in my bed. When I wake up, I check the messages on my phone to see what everyone can remember from the night before. We try to piece together what happened, usually resulting in them saying they hate me for buying the tequilas.

One of my favourite ways to persuade my friends to do anything is by texting them an inspirational message: *Where were you?* Suggesting that this night, of all nights, could be the greatest night of our lives and when we look back on it in years to come, we will ask the question, 'Where were you?' Those moments in life you can remember perfectly: Where were you when David Beckham scored THAT free kick against Greece? Where were you when Tyson Fury got up off the canvas against Deontay Wilder? And where were you when 'Agueroooooooooooo'?

13

These are the sort of 'where were you' moments I live for. Making sure I'm around friends and soaking up great, memorable atmospheres in pubs, at festivals or football matches with adrenaline pumping. The 'Where were you?' moment I definitely didn't live for is 'Where were you when you first felt a cancerous lump?' How shit is that for a memorable moment? I'm sure you'll remember your moment just as vividly.

Now, this isn't a game of tumour top trumps for who has the worst 'found your lump' story, but I'll be honest, I couldn't have been in a better place. My story began with me leaving my comfortable 9-5 in Essex working for a youth charity. I'd been offered a four month job at the Rio 2016 Olympic Games in Brazil and couldn't turn down the opportunity to work in boxing at my second Olympics. It was time to move on to the next stage of my career path.

I was comfortable in Essex but wanted to challenge myself before things like marriage, children or a mortgage might tie me down. My ex-boss, in true style, showed no emotion to me when I resigned. He didn't even attend my lunchtime leaving drinks. I'm guessing it was for fear of tearing up over my wonderful six years of service to the charity and the countless young people I'd inspired.

I wrote an emotional farewell status on Facebook telling my social media world that I'd quit my job to work at the Olympics and then after that… Quem Sabe? (Who knows). Everyone sent such supportive messages, congratulating me on taking a leap of faith, although one friend simply wrote: *Good luck catching Zika Virus.*

So, as my Grandad used to always sing to me, 'Pack up your troubles in an old kit bag and smile, smile, smile.' My six years of living in Essex were up and off I was to Brazil.

Six months before flying to Brazil, I started to learn Brazilian Portuguese on the internet with a girl living in Rio named Luciana Fernandes (who goes by the name of Luci). We communicated over WhatsApp and Skype for months teaching each other English and Brazilian Portuguese.

On my second night arriving in Brazil, I met Luci for the first time in person in Barra Shopping, the biggest shopping mall I've ever seen. We spent thirty minutes trying to find each other with neither of us being able to give directions in the other person's language. I had no idea how to say on the phone 'by the escalator on the third floor' in Brazilian Portuguese.

Eventually, our eyes connected across the shopping mall floor. As soon as Luci saw me, she sprinted towards me, jumped up and wrapped her legs around me, intertwining her ankles around my back. She covered me with multiple kisses on both cheeks just like long lost lovers. She was even more beautiful in person than over Skype. Her dark brown hair was shoulder length and she wore goofy looking glasses with huge black frames that Deidre Barlow would've been proud of. Still to this day, I've never been greeted like this by another human being in my life.

We spent the evening in an Outback restaurant in a hidden-away corner booth with red leather benches. The colour of love. Communicating only by typing into Google Translate on our phones and laughing. Luci stayed at my apartment that night and for the next two weeks after that. After three months together, we could finally talk to each other. Just about.

I've always wondered who the people are that jump into situations so positively like that. Well, Luci does. She's from another planet and says that if she's sure of something, she just knows it's right. She says a lot of her 'strange' ways of thinking are because Brazilian culture is different to British culture. That's an understatement to say the least, but she is the friendliest person you'll ever meet. Her family is from a close-knit but poor community, so she lives for music, dancing and carnival.

Luci had these Brazilian sayings that never made any sense to me like 'shut up and go', which means don't talk about doing something, just do it. The first time she told me to 'shut up and go', I took it personally, but then as time went on, it became a running joke. Luci also used to say to me 'calma' and 'relax, baby', even when I thought I was calm and relaxed. Literally, in my calmest moments on the beach, lying down, drinking a beer, she still thought I was uptight. A calm Brazilian attitude isn't on the same scale as a calm British attitude, apparently.

That year, working in Brazil, at the Rio 2016 Olympics, I had the greatest summer of my life so far. I was posting pictures on Facebook with Olympic Gold medallists, climbing the most stunning mountains and lying on golden sand beaches. I was getting one hundred likes minimum on each social media post I uploaded. The only unsettling thing about working at sports events like the Olympics is that when they finish, everyone becomes unemployed and it's a race to get the next job at the next event. Not for me though. I'd saved a couple of thousand pounds and was going to travel around South America for 3 months, racking up some more adventures, parties and credit card debts. I'd travel for as long as I could, until I got a new job or wanted to come home.

My life felt like heaven. Each morning I'd look out of my Airbnb window and could see Christ The Redeemer on one side of the apartment and Copacabana beach on the other. During the day I'd paddleboard in the bay right next to Sugar Loaf mountain, go home to get changed and then party in Lapa by the famous Lapa steps. And the Brazilians know how to party.

The Olympic games soon finished and for the first time since leaving school, I was unemployed and didn't have a base. But I was staying in a tiny apartment just next to the famous Post 5 of Copacabana beach with the most tremendous Brazilian girl I could've ever imagined. I had a flight booked to Argentina in two weeks to start my South American adventure, but Luci stopped me from leaving for an extra ten days on top of that. I'm no Brad Pitt by any stretch of the imagination, half English, half Iranian and with a big chin. I like my heritage as I'm white enough to blend in as English and dark enough to turn up to Iranian new year parties. Luci was loving my British accent, British manners and my British Passport, and that was enough for me.

I'm guessing by the fact you're reading this book you already know where you were when your life was about to get flipped upside down. You might already own a house, you might have a supportive partner, you might have a job with a regular income. I had none of these, which I think puts me in a good position to explain what happens when you don't have any or all of your Maslow's hierarchy of needs in place. Especially during a crisis such as cancer.

I was lacking a place to live, steady employment, a permanent relationship, good health and I was on the other side of the bloody world. But I was about to overcome all of that with the support of others, friendship, and the strongest mindset ever.

If you don't have a great living arrangement, we'll talk about that. If you don't have an income or financial support, we'll talk about that. If you don't have a support network and feel like you're battling alone, we'll talk about that.

So, before you head on, just sit and reflect on where you were and what you have around you now to make this journey simpler. I miss the Rio beach.

2.   Finding It

Life Lesson: Reflection is good.
Cancer Lesson: Check your balls in the shower.
Song Choice: *Don't Look Back in Anger* – Oasis

We've established 'Where were you?' will be one needless question you'll be repeatedly asked, and this will definitely be the next: 'So, how did you find your lump?' The reason I feel it's a bit pointless is because how does knowing how I found my lump contribute to me recovering from cancer? All that question does is relive the emotions I felt when I first found the lump that changed my life forever. Thanks for reminding me yet again, Grandma.

When other men ask me, 'How did you find your lump?', there's a sceptic inside me that thinks do they actually care, or do they just want to know how to check for themselves? I feel like saying, 'Don't worry, I know you just want to know how to look for a lump yourself. If you want, I can inspect you. Here, get in the shower.' Too far?

I like to imagine this as a question on an episode of *Pointless*, a BBC gameshow presented by Alexander Armstrong and Richard Osman. If you haven't watched *Pointless*, you'll need to start because if you're receiving chemotherapy or signed off work, it's usually on every day at around 5pm. Netflix, daytime TV and game shows can be your friend. *Pointless* is the show where they ask a question, and the contestants have to come up with an answer that zero people in the audience gave. Such as name a country beginning with the letter T and a pointless answer might be Turkmenistan but giving the answer as Turkey scores you seventy nine. The fewer points the better, but a pointless answer scores you the jackpot prize money.

Imagine switching on *Pointless* and Alexander Armstrong is repeating the following question to his contestants: 'We asked one hundred cancer sufferers, "How did you find your cancerous lump?" You said, "In the shower." Let's see if that's a pointless answer!'

Dududuudududlllulululululululul (the noise of the pointless gameshow machine).

'Oh noooooo, sixty seven people said "in the shower", so that is not a pointless answer. You could have had "whilst unemployed and travelling in Brazil" and that would've scored you zero points and won you todays jackpot prize.'

Richard Osman would then reel off a fact about the percentage of men who are diagnosed with testicular cancer that originally find their lump in the shower: 'The best place to check your testicles for any lumps is in a warm shower or bath. The hot water makes the skin of your scrotum relaxed so it's easy for you to use your index finger and thumb to rummage around for any painless lumps or a change in shape to your balls.'

By the way, that fact is true – the shower is the best place to check your balls. Richard Osman wouldn't lie to us like that. So, your choice of gameshows are *Pointless* or *The Chase* on ITV, but like I mentioned earlier, since performing on The *Chase* and losing £36,000 because of a question about Basil Brush, it's never been the same for me and I can no longer watch it.

When people ask me, 'Where did you find the lump?', sometimes I want to give a bizarre answer just to mix things up because answering the same question one hundred times has become tedious. People would rather ask any standard question and show interest than have any awkward silences. Like when you go on holiday and someone asks you how long the flight was. Does it matter? It's a fucking tumour. Roughly four hours to Benidorm by the way, Dave.

Occasionally, I want to reply with something spiritual like, 'I didn't find the lump, the lump found me.' It's not like I was playing some sort of trivial testicle treasure hunt where the end prize is finding a fucking tumour. The lump found me! And I'll tell you how it found me.

It was the night before the final day of the 2016 Olympic Games. The United Kingdom had just voted for Brexit, I'd just got out of the shower, and Luci was in bed. I was performing my usual towel drying routine – head, shoulders, arms, chest – and then bang!
'AHHHHHHHHHH FUCK… FUCK… FUCKING SHIT FUCK AHHHHH, I'VE BEEN STABBED, I've been fucking stabbed.'

I got out of the bathroom and my back gave away, like someone had stabbed me in the spine with a knife. No, not a knife, a Samurai sword, which had entered my back by my liver and pierced through the other side where my appendix would be.

'I'm dying!' I shouted to Luci.

'Calma baby,' she replied as she continued to watch Brazilian dance videos on her phone. I couldn't stand up any longer and laid flat on the ground so the cold apartment floor tiles were touching my back. I was desperately trying to straighten my spine and keep my legs straight. It felt like when you know cramp is about to set in, but there was a jolting reaction in my back as if I was being electrocuted across my entire body.

I just needed to get into a still position so it didn't feel like this Samurai sword was destroying my insides anymore. I've never been stabbed with a knife nor a sword, so I'm not entirely sure of the feeling, but at that moment in time I was certain this was how it felt. I felt the tile flooring cooling my back and pressed my hand into my abdomen. Like a dying soldier out of *Saving Private Ryan* who was trying to suppress the bleeding. If I moved my hand away the pain got worse. I was breathing heavily but trying to slow it down for fear of my back becoming disconnected with the cold floor and causing me further pain.

At this point Luci came over but didn't know what to do so just ran her fingers through my hair whilst looking deep into my eyes. It felt like she was trying to see if I was faking it just to get her attention away from the Brazilian dance videos. I've got a fucking Samurai sword in me, Luci, give the man some attention!

Ten minutes later, which felt like ten hours, the pain had finally gone. I couldn't believe it, the pain had just vanished. It couldn't have been muscular or skeletal and then just vanish like that. I laid there, staring up at the plain white ceiling, trying to remember what I'd eaten the night before. The pain definitely wasn't food poisoning as it was where my belt line was. Maybe my appendix had burst? I'd heard a horror story where someone's appendix burst and they died a slow and painful death, similar to those who have been impaled by a fateful Samurai sword. I anxiously got dressed but as I pulled on my jeans, there was no pain at all. Whatever it was had gone away for the day.

The next morning, I got out of the shower having totally forgotten my incident from the night before. I was standing in the bathroom drying my stomach and the bottom corner of the towel gently brushed past my testicles. It was the softest of touches and then…

'AHHHHHHHHHH FUCK… FUCK… FUCKING SHIT FUCK AHHHHH, I'VE BEEN KICKED IN THE BALLS, I've been fucking kicked in the balls.'

'Oh my God, I can't breathe, I can't breathe.' With both hands face down, I leant over the foot of the bed, my body bent at a perfect ninety-degree angle. This was the only position that relieved any pain and allowed me to find the slightest bit of comfort. I've never been stabbed by a Samurai sword, but I have been kicked in the balls before and this was definitely that feeling.

I couldn't breathe as my testicles now felt like they were up in my stomach. The pain was on par with the night before but this time it was in my left testicle. It didn't feel like my towel had brushed past me, it felt like being in the school changing rooms when someone whips up a wet towel and the end of it slaps across your backside making a cracking sound, creating a beautiful red mark on your arse. But this felt like they had aimed it directly into the middle of my left testicle. Bullseye.

I stayed in the ninety-degree bent over position for five minutes, not moving an inch and just trying to focus on breathing in and out. Then, after another five minutes, the pain just vanished. Gone again. I could jump, run, do what I liked. It couldn't be muscular or skeletal. I was now convinced I'd either burst my appendix or given myself a hernia. Neither of which I'd know how they felt or be clinically able to diagnose myself with.

It was the last day of the Olympics Games – the final medal presentations, closing ceremony for the athletes and the final goodbyes to my colleagues. I couldn't delay it any longer and decided I had to be seen by a doctor. I visited the Mediclinic in the Athletes' Village. There I was in the same Athletes Village as Usain Bolt, the fastest man in the world, alongside athletes who can jump and throw the furthest and there I was – the man with the biggest testicle. Is there a gold medal for that? Whilst all of the joys and tribulations of the final day of the Olympics were happening, I was sitting in a Mediclinic next to a French gymnast who'd horrifically broken his leg during a bad landing after a triple front flip. And little old me with a swollen testicle.

After a quick urine test, the friendly nurse said I had a urine infection and gave me an injection into my arse and two tablets for dehydration. She said that if it hadn't improved in a week then to see a doctor again. The thing is, after the Olympics finish, that's it. No more Olympics, no more Athletes' Village and no more Mediclinic. It all disappears within days. Unlike my pain, which just got worse and worse with each shower I took.

Life, God, the Universe or whatever it is you believe in came down, reminded me to never be too carefree and kicked me right in the nuts, literally. So how did I find my lump? Well, I didn't. The lump found me. The lump found me in the shower and forced me into a 90° angle over the bed feeling breathless. I'm sure you will answer this question many times to many different types of people too, and you can tell the story as dramatically or as nonchalantly as you wish, because it's your story and there are no rules.

3.   Getting A Diagnosis

Life Lesson: Sometimes you need to slow down.
Cancer Lesson: Be patient.
Song Choice: *Patience* – Take That

I know you might want to race ahead to questions like, 'How sick will I feel?' and 'What foods should I eat?' but we'll get to that. This is a slow process and all about patience. You will be drip fed information from this book, and your doctors, just like the saline that slowly drips into your blood stream (shudders with fear). If you don't have much patience, then you'll have to learn.

At the start of the cancer process you and your family will have a million questions. The doctors are the professionals who deal with this every day and now, looking back, it makes sense why they don't overload you with information. What's the point in telling you about anti-sickness pills at the start of your diagnosis when you might not take them for another month? A lot will happen in a week and your mind will be so consumed that information you are told in the morning will be a distant memory by the afternoon. Minutes of waiting for news and results will feel like hours, hours will feel like days, and days will feel like weeks.

But have patience, my friend. There is nothing more consuming in your mind during cancer and you simply have to wait, wait and wait some more. You'll wait for diagnosis tests, you'll wait for hospital appointments through the post, and you'll wait for results. If you've never been one for waiting, now's your time, and remember: Slowly is the fastest way to get to where you want to be. Sometimes it will feel like doctors and nurses are hiding information away from you or delaying appointments longer, but most of it is down to them not having the answers at that point in time. Life has told you to slowwwww down and you must listen. No more rushing to work to be on time, no more rushing to catch a train, no more rushing to live up to society's expectations. Slow down! Just for now, anyway.

You know the saying: 'Good things come to those who wait'? Well, it's not exactly the case with a cancer diagnosis, is it? The best thing that could come from waiting is the doctor turning round and saying, 'You won't believe it, but we've only gone and made a mistake. You don't have cancer, now be on your way and enjoy the rest of your life.'

That doesn't happen. Getting a diagnosis is one of the slowest phases of cancer. It's not uncommon for a few misdiagnoses to take place along the way too. Going doctor to doctor until the problem is sorted because a cancer pain will never just leave you alone. A week after my misdiagnosis of 'being dehydrated' by the Olympic Village Mediclinic, the pain in my testicle still hadn't gone away. The testicle was now starting to get bigger, and I was fearful it could be a twisted testicle. I've seen some horrific pictures of a friend that had a twisted testicle, and they say it can even cause death. I still wasn't worried about it being cancer because I knew that a cancer symptom is a painless pea-shaped lump growing on your testicle. I didn't have any painless peas growing on my balls, I just had a ball getting bigger and bigger, and more and more pain.

I later found out the reason for this was that my pea-shaped lump was growing bigger from inside my ball. The bastard. It didn't exactly feel like it was pea-sized. Certainly not a petit-pois anyway. I used to have nice little plums but now leftie was growing to be an evil coconut.

Luci and I travelled from our Copacabana apartment to a clinic in the city district of Rio, away from downtown and the beaches. We waited in a tiny room, which contained nothing but three plastic chairs, before being called into the doctor's room. We could barely enter the even tinier doctor's room. It felt like if there were any more doors to open, we'd keep shrinking into some Willy Wonka mystery tour. The doctor didn't speak much English but took a look at my balls and started speaking to Luci in Brazilian Portuguese. Now, I'd been learning to speak the language for a few months so I could converse but when two Brazilians are talking together at a rapid pace, I had no chance. I heard three things that I recognised in the conversation: 'muito problemo', 'tumour' and 'gonorrhoea'.

As Luci and I left the doctor's clinic, he gave me a paper bag full of condoms which confused me even further. I was hung up on the word 'gonorrhoea'.

'I thought you said I was your only partner and you'd been tested?' I waved the pack of condoms in my hand as we hurried to catch the metro back to Copacabana.

'Yes, I told you this.' Luci raged at me as she started walking faster and faster.

'So why did he say gonorrhoea and then give me a packet of condoms?'

'They tested you for gonorrhoea and STIs and you don't have it,' Luci said, almost at jogging pace now. Relieved, my shoulders started to relax back to a normal level. 'But... you might have a tumour,' she mumbled with her head down as she sped off.

A what? A fucking tumour? Surely that's a bad thing and all the doctor had given me was a bag of condoms. I was in disbelief. Never in my life have I been so disappointed to hear that I DIDN'T have gonorrhoea. If these were the only two options, then I didn't like this game very much.

We got the metro back to our apartment in Copacabana and just held hands the whole way without speaking to each other. I couldn't find any words to say in English, let alone any words in Brazilian Portuguese. The doctor must've been the equivalent of a GP and I would need to see a consultant for a scan to find out what was really going on.

I couldn't find a consultant in Rio that had any available appointments so I was going to wait until I got to Argentina as I was flying in just two days. I had been working with Argentinians and Brazilians at the Olympic Games and we'd always had great banter, such as who was better out of Maradona and Pele? Lionel Messi was better than Neymar. Argentinian steak and wine was more delicious than Brazil's. I couldn't wait to try these things when I got there. But now the only question I was interested in was: Who had the best consultants to detect possible tumours?

4.   Benign Or Malignant?

Life Lesson: You don't know what you've got 'till it's gone.

Cancer Lesson: If you want answers, you need questions.

Song Choice: *Big Yellow Taxi* – Counting Crows

Denial... It's not just a river in Africa. It's hard to accept or comprehend that you have a life-threatening disease when you only have a small lump or an infrequent pain. It's also a lot easier and much more convenient to just ignore things and get on with life, especially when you don't feel particularly ill day to day. You can't go to the doctor every time you have a slight knock, bad cough or painful stomach, scared it's cancer, as you'd be spending all of your time visiting hospitals. So, why didn't you get checked earlier?

There's a whole heap of reasons: Timing. Fear. Too busy. Denial. Or a combination of the lot. You don't simply have a test for cancer and then a doctor tells you the diagnosis directly with no fluff. It's not like that at all.

Doctors can tell us confusing information, perhaps with an assumption that we know exactly what they're talking about. Or do they expect us to go away and do our own research? The multiple consultations take some getting used to so it's important to ask any questions you want answers to. You might only have ten minutes with a consultant before their next appointment so make sure you have your questions ready. Write them down on a piece of paper or your phone if you have to. Be honest and open.

There's no time to waste, you could be dying here. This day will probably mark the first day of the rest of your life. This was the case for me as I've never had a bigger U-turn in 24 hours.

I woke up at 4am on Friday morning, shivering, sweating and shaking. Luci hugged me tightly in bed and said that I was just nervous about flying to Argentina and she quickly fell back to sleep. I downed a handful of what I hoped was painkillers in preparation for my next shower and any potential encounters with a Samurai sword. This feeling was more than nerves; was it a panic attack? My body was telling me something I needed to listen to. So, during my sleepless night, I booked an appointment at the nearby Galdino Campos Private Clinic. I sat awake, scrolling my phone, until Luci woke up again at 9am. She agreed today was the day we'd sort out Evil Jose, the nickname she'd given to my lump. She was the first person to ever personify one of my balls, but this gave me confidence that we had him outnumbered. Fuck you, Jose.

The appointment was at 4pm and cost me £400 of my travelling money for the pleasure. Luci and I arrived at the clinic and were welcomed into a room by Dr. Ronaldo Galdino Campos. Yes, the owner of the clinic and what an awesome name. He didn't look much like a Ronaldo. More of a Brian. Dr. Campos was in his fifties with a bald head, glasses and a white lab coat. He looked like a scientist. Dr. Campos asked me to take down my shorts and began to inspect my evil testicle Jose. Dr. Ronaldo Galdino Campos has a fantastic name and clearly knows his way around a testicle.

'You MUST get a scan before you leave Brazil,' Dr. Campos insisted as I pulled my shorts and pants back up. He picked up his phone and swiftly called a nearby hospital and asked for an emergency appointment. 'Usually, they don't have appointments for at least a week, but my friend Dr. Perpétuo has agreed to see you tonight at 7pm.' Although Dr. Campos hadn't given me any answers, he was very direct in where I would find them. He took me to one of the treatment rooms where a nurse hooked me up to an IV drip for an hour to make me feel better. As I lay in bed, with a tube coming out of my hand, Luci fell asleep with her head by my feet.

Luci and I left the Galdino Campos Clinic and walked twenty-minutes to the Copa D'or Hospital. We arrived fifteen-minutes before 7pm and were greeted on arrival by Dr Daniel Perpétuo, who called us directly into his office. Dr. Daniel Perpétuo is a real-life dreamboat. He has the aura of the coolest doctor in town. When he walks through the corridors, everyone's heads turn as he passes by. He introduced himself in perfect English.

'Hello Afsheen, I'm your doctor, call me Daniel.' So approachable. Dr. Perpétuo, sorry, I mean Dr. Daniel. He had Action Man hair and wore his white lab coat with panache; the seams stretched by his muscles. I bet when he's not saving lives, he's down the beach in tiny speedos playing beach volleyball. I bet he looks fantastic doing that as well. Dr. Daniel rubbed his hands together to bring them to the perfect temperature, inspected Evil Jose and instantly said he would send me for an ultrasound scan right away. Dr. Daniel didn't have time to conduct the ultrasound himself because he was about to go into theatre.

He was probably off to perform a heart bypass and then deliver a set of twins in the maternity ward on the way back. What a guy!

'I'll see you later tonight to discuss the results but ONLY if you require further treatment. If the ultrasound results come back ok, then I'll just phone you because it's getting late and my shift finishes soon.' With that, Dr. Daniel left me with his doctors and a nurse who painfully inserted a cannula into my hand. The nurse spoke zero English and could have been inserting anything into me, but this was a time for trust. I took a picture of the cannula in my hand and jokingly posted it to my Instagram story with the caption #PrayForAf.

As we returned to the waiting room, Luci had to leave me to go to a university lecture. She'd missed this lecture three Fridays in a row because every Friday was supposed to be my last weekend in Brazil. The university was now threatening to throw her off the course if she missed a fourth week. We didn't want her to lose her place on the course, so she went across town to her class and would come back afterwards.

I sat alone in the waiting room and eventually a young doctor with shaggy hair called me into the ultrasound room. I'd had an ultrasound scan before on my stomach for potential pancreatitis, so I knew what to expect. An obstetric ultrasound is what they use to look at a foetus during a baby scan and a medical ultrasound is used for internal body images that X-rays can't pick up. It's the same machine that scans both. Well, not the same machine, that would be weird, but you know what I mean.

The young Scooby Doo, shaggy-haired looking doctor asked me to take my shorts down and lie on the bed. He applied the blue gel onto the handheld scanning device, and I laid there flat with my arms stiff by my side. The blue gel is ice cold, and gives you a jolting feeling when it first touches your balls, similar to when a doctor hasn't warmed up their stethoscope. It's like wading into the sea or a cold swimming pool – that moment when the cold water first touches your balls and takes your breath away.

By the way, the cold feeling on the testicles is because the testes are the coldest part of your anatomy at thirty-five degrees Celsius. Sperm needs to be kept at a cooler temperature than your thirty-seven degrees body temperature, so that's why they exist in a sack outside of your body. Think of it as your body's fridge compartment to keep the plums fresh and the sperm working. So, men, you are right to walk sheepishly into the sea and cold swimming pools.

Dr. Shaggy swivelled his chair round, holding the hand-held device like a supermarket cashier about to price up a pair of plums through the till. First, he rolled the handheld device over my beautiful healthy right testicle and captured all of the images on the computer screen. I was looking at the screen over my shoulder like a proud parent watching the ultrasound and heartbeat of my unborn baby. He scanned on the top of the ball, to the right of the ball and then underneath. Ok that looks normal, now let's see how Evil Jose compares.

Doctor Shaggy applied more blue jelly to the device and I felt another cold jolting feeling to my left testicle. He lifted both testicles like a supermarket cashier searching for the barcode on a sack of satsumas. He scanned Evil Jose on the top of the ball, to the left of it and then underneath. I kept my eyes on the screen throughout. It looked exactly the same! Both scans looked exactly the fucking same. I'm out of trouble here, I've dodged a bullet yet again, I know it.

'Uno momento, por favor.' Dr. Shaggy walked out of the room for less than a minute and returned with his supervisor. The doctor came in like the supermarket supervisor who had just been called to the till because there's an unexpected item in the baggage area. The supervisor was an older doctor with a similar shaggy haircut, but more Paul Weller than Shaggy. Dr. Paul Weller repeated the procedure – cold jelly, ball scan to righty, cold jelly, ball scan to Evil Jose – before saying something to Dr. Shaggy in Brazilian Portuguese way too fast for me to understand.

'Is everything ok?' I asked the older and wiser doctor as I pulled up my shorts.

'Dr. Daniel will speak with you in his room'

'Urmmm, alright. Am I ok to leave then?'

'Dr. Daniel will speak with you in his room, it's for the best,' he repeated once more.

I turned to Dr. Shaggy and he put one hand on my shoulder.

'My friend… it's all going to be ok.' And then hugged me. He fucking HUGGED ME!

Arms around me and cuddling me. Was this another part of Brazilian culture I didn't know? Doctors in Brazil seem much friendlier than British ones, that's for sure. As I left the embrace, I gave him the double tap on his back just to show it was a manly hug and nothing romantic.

I returned to the waiting room totally confused and still with the cannula in my hand. Why had a doctor just hugged me? As the time passed, I kept thinking, where is Dr. Daniel? He said if there was a problem, he would see me tonight and tell me. There's no sign of him anywhere and he wouldn't let me down like this. Either he's been delayed saving another life or he's gone home because he knows there's nothing to worry about and I'll be drinking wine in Buenos Aires this time tomorrow.

Dr. Daniel also mentioned that if I needed surgery then the treatment was all free of charge. Bargain! But if it wasn't serious enough for surgery, then it would be £400 for the consultation and £700 for the ultrasound. Jesus, my travelling money could be cut in half in the space of three hours. I started to think the only way I could afford to travel South America was if they did perform a FREE surgery on my testicle. What a predicament. A few days ago, I was caught between having a tumour or gonorrhoea, and today the options were spending fifteen hundred pounds or having one less testicle. It was a terrible game of Would You Rather?

The time dragged on longer and fewer nurses were now patrolling the hospital floors. Still no sign of Dr. Daniel. Then wise old Dr. Paul Weller appeared again and called me into an office.

'Is your friend Luci on her way back to the hospital?' He took a seat and pointed to the chair opposite for me to sit in.

'No, she's still at university.'

36

'Ok, I am going to phone her and tell her not to come back tonight.'

It must be good news! Dr. Daniel must have gone home because everything is fine, and Dr. Paul Weller is calling Luci to tell her not to return so I'm out of here. Even Dr. Shaggy told me it was all going to be ok and hugged me goodbye. I sat there smiling because I knew I had been let off the hook; the cat had fallen on his feet once again. *Hola Argentina dos vinos por favor!* I always ride my luck and I had come up trumps once more. The big digital clock on the wall changed from 9:36 to 9:37pm, the room stunk of bleach and disinfectant, and Dr. Paul Weller's face dropped…

'Mr Afsheen … It's… a tumour. The results show you've got a nodule in your testicle.' The doctor sat there with no emotion on his face but his eyes pierced sympathetically into mine as if I should have been sad.

'We'll need to do a biopsy to test if it is benign or malignant.'

I nearly shrugged it off and said, 'Ahh, at least it's not cancer.' But I thought, he's not used the word cancer so let's not be dramatic.

'Urmmmm, what's a nodule?' I asked instead.

'It's a small lump that can be a tumour.' He wheeled his chair closer to me.

'Right, ok so how bad is it?'

'Dr. Daniel has asked you to come back tomorrow for surgery and to do further tests.'

He put one hand on my knee and gave me a half-raised smile before walking out and leaving me on my own.

A conveyor belt of thoughts began in my brain: Benign, malignant, nodule? I don't know what any of these words mean. Are they English or Brazilian Portuguese? Why's he looking so sad? I know a tumour has something to do with cancer, but is it cancer? He hasn't mentioned cancer so maybe it's not that bad. Should I start crying? I think benign means dead and malignant doesn't sound great, but either way, if it's a tumour, surely I don't want a benign or malignant one inside me. It's not exactly the defining moment I was expecting. More confusing than anything.

This was my first taste of a diagnosis and my first judgement day. It's not the bombshell 'moment of truth' you crave but it is vividly memorable. You'll remember what the doctor wore, what time it was, the smells, the feelings, the anxiety. We're told in so many ways that we could have a tumour with words we don't recognise in English let alone in Portuguese. The word 'tumour' is universal to nearly every single language on the planet. That's how shit they are. So... I was told I might have a benign or malignant nodule, where a nodule is a lump, where lumps can be tumours, where tumours can be cancer, and I needed a biopsy, and I needed surgery, and cancer can spread, and cancer can kill you and and and and MAKE IT STOP!

Am I going to die or not? Do I need to speed up the completion of my bucket list and book a skydive? I knew from my university days that a biopsy involved extracting body tissue for examination. Surely, they wouldn't do that to my poor testicle? Come to think of it, any surgery on my testicle was going to cause me pain for days or weeks and

I was about to stay in a five dollar a night party hostel in a sixteen-bed dorm in Buenos Aires. I sat on my own in Copa D'or Hospital, just eight hundred metres away from the glorious Copacabana beach but five thousand six hundred and fifty eight miles away from my home. It felt even further.

5.   Goodbye Normal

Life Lesson: Life can change in a day.
Cancer Lesson: You must remember to eat.
Song Title: *Roll With It* – Oasis

As I write this, over three years on from my first day of a diagnosis, I realise that was my last day of 'normal'. I won't tell you how tumorous cells develop or the science of how chemotherapy works, but I will give you facts about cancer, chemo and cannulas along the way. I also want to bring attention to the fears and complete chaos that cancer brings to friendships and family. I was a naive twenty-nine-year-old before cancer. We had no previous family history of cancer, so I thought it just involved getting a diagnosis, some chemo, losing your hair and then you recover, or you don't. That isn't even the half of it. It has some life-lasting effects, and you have to find a new normal. Everyone has different reactions to a crisis or trauma, and not just the cancer sufferers themselves. Everyone is affected, sometimes others more so than the person who is actually sick.

I left Copa D'or Hospital and they gave me Dr. Daniel's personal mobile number so that I could phone him to arrange an appointment time. Oh, and before I could get emotional, I had to pay a medical bill of £1,100 on the way out just for an extra kick in the nuts.

I shuffled slowly onto the busy streets of Rio and then it hit me. The busy taxis and bright lights became a total blur as my eyes started to fill with tears. It was now

10pm in Brazil and 2am back in the UK. There was no one I could call at this time of night and the loneliness kicked in. I sank to my knees. It was the loneliest place on Earth. I was so alone I felt sick with emptiness.

The fast pace of a Friday night in Rio doesn't stop for anyone sobbing on their knees on the side of the street. My eyes were full of tears, but I still wasn't actually crying, just sobbing. I started to heave, and my hands started sweating. I could feel I was about to be sick. Suddenly, my phone pinged, and I saw that Luci had sent me a message. My legs went to jelly and I couldn't walk any further in a straight line. I sat on the pavement and started to message Luci across WhatsApp. The doctor had phoned her whilst she was in her class and told her about my diagnosis because he could explain it better to her in Portuguese.

I wiped away my blurry eyes and focussed on what Luci was typing…

Luci: *Tomorrow we need to see him in his clinic to explain for you.*
Af: *But did he tell you why? I'm going to cry and feel sick.*
Luci: *I'm in class, be calm.*
Af: *The doctor told me what's wrong…*
Luci: *Yes me too, and the next thing to do… Do you know as well?*
Af: *He said surgery.*
Luci: *Do you wanna Subway sandwich?*
Af: *I don't think you understand.*
Luci: *Yes, I understood.*
Luci: *But you need to relax now.*

Did I want a Subway sandwich? The most defining moment at the saddest, loneliest time of my life so far. Tears on the streets of Rio and the first thing that anyone asks me is: Do you want a Subway sandwich? I couldn't believe it. I paused for over a minute, staring at the message. I wondered if there had been a language barrier, but maybe Luci was right. No sobbing, crying, or being upset and sitting on a pavement would fix anything. I was panicking about what the diagnosis of a tumour might mean, but all Luci wanted to know was if I'd like my Subway toasted and with cheese. I had to be calm and I still had to eat.

I eventually got a taxi back to my apartment and Luci was waiting for me on the doorstep with a plastic bag in her hand. She'd bought me the 'sub of the day'. I'll never look at a twelve-inch meatball mariana in the same way ever again. I still couldn't bring myself to eat it but picked at the cookies instead.

We took the elevator to the tenth floor and in my apartment I laid on the bed, staring at the ceiling again. This was becoming a familiar sight from the depths of despair: looking at ceilings for the answers. Then my phone pinged with a WhatsApp message. It was Dr. Daniel! I love you, man. He'd texted me at 10:30pm on his night off. What a lovely fantastic, handsome man you are, Dan. Although, if a doctor's messaging you on WhatsApp at 10:30pm on a Friday night, it's not going to be good news is it? I was still in a state of confusion about what to do next. He wanted to see me the next day, but I had my flight booked to Argentina and no accommodation booked in Rio. I had a whole load of questions so began to message him…

Dr. Daniel: *Mr Afsheen, Sorry I did not get a chance to see you but come to the hospital tomorrow and we can discuss further. What is a good time?*

Af: *Hi Daniel, Thanks for the message. I can come in the morning, but I am supposed to be flying to Argentina and now I don't know what to do.*

Dr. Daniel: *Yes, it is difficult news to hear. I understand.*

Af: *The doctor said it's a tumour but then he said I have a nodule. What is the difference?*

Dr. Daniel: *A nodule is a tumour. It can get bigger so we need to do more tests and it could take some time to recover.*

Af: *I am on the internet now looking at flights back to England. I might just go home?*

Dr. Daniel: *Yes, honestly, I think it would be the best option for you.*

Af: *Ok, I'm going to book a flight then and I will call you in the morning.*

Dr. Daniel: *Afsheen, this is the right decision. Don't worry, everything will be ok in the end.*

So, Dr. Daniel told me it was best to go home. Maybe South America wasn't my destiny this time, plus I'd now spent most of my travelling money before I even started. I went straight onto the internet for the next available flight to London and it was for 9pm the next night. Rio de Janiero direct to London for £1,850. Economy. Fuck it! An eleven-hour flight to ponder what else I could have spent over £3,000 on within one day. Well, it's only money and you can't take it with you when you die, can you? And at this point the Grim Reaper was creeping up on me as the days went on. My body went into flight or fight mode and I decided I was going to fight this thing. Well, after I took a flight, of course. ELEVEN HOURS!

Luci and I went to bed and watched the movie *Deadpool*, not talking much just holding each other. Before I received my tumour news, I had this feeling that I'd go travelling and miss Luci so much that I'd have to return to Rio and we'd live happily ever after. We'd have Brazilian babies and call them Af Junior, Afsheenio and Afizinho. They'd grow up to be talented footballers, not quite good enough to play for Brazil but they'd give it a good go in the England squad.

I woke up early Saturday morning and couldn't sleep again so brought Luci breakfast in bed from her favourite café. We reluctantly packed my backpack at a snail's pace, and she kept five of my unwashed shirts to remember me by. Luci had to catch a bus back to her mum's house, so left me before it was my time to depart. We stood at the front door of my apartment and hugged and kissed not wanting to leave each other for the very last time.

She scuttled across the corridor and pressed the button for the elevator. As she waited for the elevator to come to the tenth floor, she looked back and ran towards me like the first time we met in the shopping centre. She grabbed the back of my head with both hands, stared deeply into my eyes and gave me the biggest, wettest kiss. The elevator pinged and opened its doors and she ran towards it. As she reached the elevator, the doors began to close, and she trapped it open with her foot and the doors opened wide again. She turned back to me once more and shouted, 'Af... Shut up and go.'

I didn't know whether to laugh or cry. This girl had entered my life in the most dramatic fashion I'd ever experienced and now she'd left with the most emotional exit. It wasn't as if she lived around the corner; it was an eleven-hour flight! Is that it forever? I started to feel guilty. She'd only signed up to a languages website to learn some English. She didn't know it would end up like this. As I shut the door of my apartment behind me, I wondered if I'd see her ever again.

6.   It's Coming Home

Life Lesson: A cup of tea can solve everything.
Cancer Lesson: Honesty is the best policy.
Song Choice: *Not Nineteen Forever* – The Courteeners

So, at this point, I had a possible benign malignant nodule tumour lump. Whatever that meant.

For the record, benign means not harmful in effect, whereas malignant means very virulent or infectious. A nodule is an abnormal tissue growth, and a tumour is a mass of diseased cells that might become a lump or cause illness. In short, a benign nodule = not so good. A malignant tumour = very bad.

Now is the time you might start to tell people close to you. I say 'might' because I was shocked by how many men have since told me they faced their cancer without telling anyone. The stories were bizarre for me to hear but everyone has their reasons.

A friend's dad had prostate cancer and got all the way to the point of chemotherapy before telling his wife and children. He was fearful of upsetting his wife and felt like he was the man of the house so had to remain tough with a stiff upper lip. But cancer doesn't care for stiff upper lips. The first rule of cancer club is: 'It's ok to talk about cancer.'

Men may have a tendency to not tell their families, but this can cause major implications. Just look what happened to Walter White when he kept his new diagnosis to himself. He went on to become one of the biggest drug barons in

America, orchestrate his brother-in law's shooting and cause the murder of multiple people. If he'd just told his wife and family at the start maybe none of that would have happened. If you got that reference to Breaking Bad (one of the greatest TV drama series of all time), then great. If you haven't seen Breaking Bad, well, now you'll have time to watch every series. It's a classic. Everyone's going to react differently no matter how you tell them. Trust me, this is where it gets weird.

Once Luci had left me, I started preparing for my journey home. Sorting out my backpack whilst singing, 'Pack up your troubles in an old kit bag and smile, smile, smile.'

After I'd packed everything, I had one last stroll along the Copacabana promenade looking out at the excitement of Rio one last time. I'd always dreamt of travelling to Brazil since watching Ronaldo at the 1998 World Cup. I was infatuated with Brazil. I had a Brazilian flag as a towel, I listened to Brazilian music and I wore Brazilian pants. I even nearly changed my name as a child by deed poll to Denilson, because I didn't like my name Afsheen. I never imagined it would end up like this.

I got an Uber to Rio International Airport and as I arrived, the queue for the British Airways check-in was a huge snaking line – one I was going to be standing in for at least an hour. It was strange because I knew I had a tumour, but no one else did. It's not like I was wearing a badge with 'tumour on board' as my lump was still not showing. I wondered if a member of the BA staff would maybe give me fast-track priority boarding, or perhaps even bump me up into first class if I told them I had a tumour. I spent thirty minutes telling myself that I'd tell the check-in attendant I had a tumour. I even had a letter from the hospital to prove it. I finally got to the front of the desk and suddenly thought, *What if they don't let people fly with a tumour and I get stuck here in Brazil?* So, I bottled it. I couldn't play the cancer card just yet.

Nobody knew I was flying home to the UK apart from Dad. Everyone, including Mum, thought I was having the time of my life, partying in Brazil. I sat in the departures lounge and decided to text my mate Turton to tell him I was coming home. It was Saturday night back in England and he text me straight back.

IM FfuCking Pished geez.

Ok, maybe this wasn't a good time to confide in Turton.

I sent a message to another mate Pete and he texted me straight back too.

What do you want you fucking prick?

And then sent me a picture of a table full of empty pint glasses. Ok, Pete could wait as well.

Before travelling to Brazil, my younger brother, Parsa had morbidly told me how many planes had crashed from Brazil to the UK. As I boarded the gigantic Airbus A380 and sat in my window seat 32J, a fear of flying suddenly kicked in. Maybe it was down to my brother's scare tactics, but it was more likely due to my new heightened sense of mortality. I thought, *This will be just my luck, I'll die in a plane crash and my body will never be recovered in the Atlantic Ocean.*

And when Mum finds out I was only flying home for an untreated tumour, I think it would be safe to say my time was up.

Suddenly, I wanted to tell my best mates John and George my news because I'd convinced myself that the plane would plummet into the ocean resulting in my certain death. Before I could construct a reasonable message to the lads, the flight captain announced for cabin crew to take their seats for take-off and that all phones should be switched to airplane mode. I was about to embark on an eleven-hour flight with no WI-FI and no one to talk to. I was about to be forced into overthinking with no distractions. I stared down the aisle of the plane – why hadn't I used the cancer card to get into first class?

I opened up my Football Manager game on my phone and played it for the next six hours, taking Southampton to Premier League and European glory, whilst deservedly winning Manager of the Year. Show me another football manager that could win those sorts of accolades with a newly diagnosed tumour.

ELEVEN HOURS later (have I mentioned the flight was eleven hours yet?), I landed in London. The greatest city in the world. God Save the Queen, I was back in blighty. I phoned Dad and he was predictably running late. It's a three-hour drive from Weymouth to London Heathrow and it was a rare occurrence for him to pick me up as he hated the drive. Although it was a pleasant day for September in England, it was no Rio weather. My feet were bitterly cold but that was down to my choice of wearing Haviana flip-flops for arrival, which screamed out, 'I've been on holiday!'

I left the terminal and saw Dad running across the zebra crossing with a trolley. He took my backpack from me – it was nearly as tall as him making him look like a giant tortoise. Dad was in his usual smart trousers and shirt. He put my backpack onto the trolley and pushed it quickly to the short-stay car park. There was no chance he was getting a parking fine or paying more than the minimum payment.

I'd asked Dad to pick me up because it had been easier to tell him about my problem for some reason. Probably due to the knowledge he wouldn't start crying. I knew it was going to be a lot harder telling Mum. She'd only have worried if I'd told her over the phone, so Dad agreed to pick me up and take me to Mum's house.

As we got closer to the car, I noticed the windows on his Mercedes were down. It didn't make sense because it was cold but as I got closer, I smelt the cigarettes and realised he was trying to disguise the smell of his last Marlboro Red. Dad's always denied being a smoker and says he only smokes when he has a drink or if he's stressed. I think he's stressed four days a week and alleviates that stress by drinking on the other three.

Dad didn't ask about my balls. He's never asked about them before so how would he know how to bring them up? We've never spoken about things like that to be honest. I wouldn't say Dad is emotionless, far from it. He just has a different way of showing it. I say 'showing it' in the loosest sense of the words.

He grew up in Iran as the oldest of seventeen siblings. He has six brothers and ten sisters. I can't imagine he made much of an emotional connection with his dad as he would've been busy with the other sixteen children that came along. To my knowledge, there weren't many mental health campaigns encouraging men to talk openly about their problems in Iran in the sixties. Dad worked on a family farm picking tea leaves and oranges before fleeing Iran at sixteen years old to come to England. He got a degree, married Mum, and worked as an architect. When I was six years old Mum and Dad split up.

Then one day, when I was twelve years old, I opened the local newspaper to see that Dad had opened a new gentleman's lap dancing club in town. I became the popular kid in school overnight. Not only with my fellow students but also with my teachers and football coaches. There are probably less interesting experiences when accompanying your dad on a 'Bring Your Son to Work' day. The jury is still out on if I actually passed my geography GCSE or if Mr Collins bumped up my coursework grade after Dad winked at him on a parent's evening and said, 'Hello Steve.' Growing up with your dad owning a lap-dancing club has its experiences, but that's a story for another time.

Dad and I stopped on the M3 motorway at Fleet service station for a KFC. The first meals I have when returning to the UK are a KFC box meal and a Chinese takeaway. Good old English grub. No one knew I was back in England, so I walked around the service station with my cap pulled down hiding my face, like some shamed celeb trying to avoid getting papped by photographers. Even though we were still two hours from home, I didn't want someone to see me and report back to Mum that I was at

Fleet service station, when I was supposed to be in South America.

We continued the drive to Dorset, and finally over the summit of Ridgeway Hill, which overlooks the view of Weymouth and Portland. That's always when I feel like I'm truly home. When I see that view and the sun is shining on Weymouth, I feel like Simba looking over Pride Rock in the Lion King, the clouds hanging over Portland like the forbidden elephant graveyard.

The journey took close to four hours and we didn't speak about my tumour once. The word cancer certainly wasn't used. We spoke about Roy Hodgson's departure as the England Manager, what might happen now the United Kingdom had voted to leave the European Union, and Donald Trump's chances of winning the upcoming US election. Anything but tumours.

We arrived at Mum's and I noticed her car wasn't parked on the driveway. As we got closer, I realised my grandparents' car was parked there instead. They were obviously visiting for the day and also didn't know I was coming home. 'Great, that's all I need', I thought. 'I'm going to break Grandma's heart and probably give Grandad a coronary'.

Dad and I unloaded my bags. I didn't have a key to the house so knocked on the door, which was quickly unlocked by Grandma. Rather than her usual greeting joke of, 'Not today, thank you', she opened the door wide.

'Oh, the wanderer returns,' she announced to the house.

We carefully navigated the bags and ourselves through the door – there was barely any room for two people to cross paths – and plonked my luggage into the living room, surprising Mum and Grandad.

Grandad was sitting in the one-seater leather armchair because he doesn't like the three-seater sofa that smells of dogs and is covered in horsehair. He was fiddling with a horse's whip that Mum had left lying around in the now cramped living room. Grandad is the joker of the family and the acorn of our great oak tree. He's always laughing and telling amazing stories. Grandma is like the Queen of England but without the expensive pearls or crown. She was ecstatic that I was home and Grandad started pretending he was orchestrating a brass band with the horse's whip whilst humming The Dam Busters tune out the side of his mouth. They always worried when I travelled and had formed their opinion of Brazil from watching negative news about gun crime and the spread of the Zika virus. However, now I was safely back home in one piece, they thought.

I sat in the middle of the three-seater sofa with Grandma on my right and Dad on my left. Grandad was sprawled out on the armchair and Mum stood in front of the television just in front of us all as if she'd taken centre stage to break into song to perform to the crowd.

'I suppose you've run out of money then?' Mum smirked like she was cracking an opening joke to the audience at a stand-up comedy gig.

'Oh, I expect he was just missing his mum too much.' Grandma held onto my hands, sandwiching them between her two palms to warm them up.

'He's probably been deported,' Grandad joked mid-hum whilst now orchestrating with his left-hand, signalling to the imaginary percussionists in the back row.

'Not quite… umm… I went to the doctors in Rio and they said they found a tumour, so I've had to fly home.' I felt my body nearly vanish into the cracks of the sofa. I wanted to disappear and for the sofa to swallow me whole.

It was silent for a couple of seconds; even Grandad's brass band had stopped playing,

'Oh well, at least you're home safe now.' Grandma began rubbing my hands faster in between hers.

'Right, umm… ok … who wants a cup of tea then?' Mum pointed at us like a waitress taking orders in a café.

Mum took the orders and went into the kitchen with Grandma. It was the longest cup of tea I've ever waited for. It's true what they say – a watched pot never boils. For over ten minutes we waited. I was guessing maybe Mum and Grandma were crying in the kitchen. *They must be*, I thought. *I've told five people now and all I've been offered is a Subway sandwich and a cup of tea, and not one person has cried. Someone give me your tears.*

The atmosphere in the living room was getting tense with Grandad just turning up the volume of Dad's Army on the TV. Every now and then he'd turn to look at me as if he didn't know what to say. Then right on cue, Captain Mannering shouted to his corporal, 'You stupid boy, Pike!' and Grandad glanced at me once more. Mum and Grandma finally returned with cups of lukewarm tea, a side plate of chocolate digestives, and red eyes.

'Don't worry, it's only a tumour, it's probably nothing,' I said as I dunked my first chocolate digestive into my cup of tea. The tea not quite hot enough to melt the chocolate like it usually does. 'I have a doctor's appointment at 11 am on Monday morning so no point worrying until then. Oh, and Mum… can I move back into my old room?'

7.   You Have Two Options

Life Lesson: You always have two options.
Cancer Lesson: A diagnosis is good.
Song Choice: *Three Little Birds* – Bob Marley

The day no one wants to experience and the news no one wants to hear. This is where everything speeds up to one-hundred miles per hour if it hasn't felt like that already. A lot can happen in twenty-four hours. Strangely though, I think this day brings a tiny drop of relief. But how can someone be relieved they've got cancer?

Getting a diagnosis can be a lengthy process. You might have been told so many times that, 'It could be... but it's probably nothing to worry about...', when deep down you know you aren't well. With a confirmed diagnosis you enter the system and once you're in the system, it's all spaceships are go.

You are always in control of your emotions and now all of that society expectation bullshit that people get dragged into doesn't even show up on your radar. Climbing the career ladder, petty arguments, finding a partner – it all becomes secondary. You just want to be healthy again. Your survival mode is activated. You know something bad is happening to you, but you also HAVE to believe you can overcome it.

Get ready for the changes. Day by day and sometimes hour by hour, your life is going to take drastic turns. By becoming mentally aware of the changes sooner you can move from denial and anger into acceptance, and then you can take action. You'll be able to watch yourself, and others around you, move through these emotions. You'll watch people live out these stages, play by play to the book, and it's quite fascinating to watch.

As the sufferer, you might think this will affect you the most emotionally, but for me that wasn't the case. I'd sat on the eleven-hour flight from Brazil and moved from denial (the diagnosis was wrong!) to anger that the tumour had ruined my plans. Then I accepted what it was and began exploring the ways I could beat this shit. For others around me it didn't happen as fast.

Dad had made an appointment with Dr. Evans at our local GP surgery at 11am. I'd been registered to the surgery since I was a child, so they'd known me for years. Previous medical history included asthma, problematic knees and a case of the mumps.

On that Monday morning, Dad and I parked in the underground carpark and took the old brick staircase with the red bannister to the surgery. Being a true germophobe, I'd never touched that bannister in all my years of visiting. We reached the second floor and were greeted by the ever-friendly receptionist. This is sarcasm. The way this receptionist always asks for my symptoms before I arrive is like she wishes she was the doctor. This time I was ready for her patronising questions and was going to knock her off her feet.

'Yes, what is it today?' she asked whilst not even lifting her head to engage eye contact.

'I've got a tumour.' She stopped taking notes and looked up at me slowly. She smiled and raised her eyebrows as if to say sorry and convey shock at the same time.

'Urmm, Dr Evans is ready for you now Mr Panj …allliii …zarrrr …daayyyyy. Down the corridor second door on the right.'

I knew exactly where his room was. She knew that I knew where his room was. Maybe she was feeling guilty and that I deserved an improved level of hospitality now that I had a 'real illness'. At least she'd attempted to say my surname for once.

Dr. Evans is a positive doctor, maybe too positive at times. I think you could walk in with your head missing, and he'd prescribe some rest and a course of paracetamol and say you'll be back to work in three to five days. He has a conveyor belt of patients in and out of his room all day long. His office hasn't changed in over twenty-nine years of appointments and I know to stay seated until I get a prescription or recommended to a consultant.

I sat down on the black chair with mahogany armrests, and a waft of air blew out from the side of the old leather, the *pfftttt* sound also releasing the stench of old people. The examination table was covered in blue roll paper similar to industrial kitchen roll and there was a matching blue curtain screen. His cabinets were loaded with all sorts of medical instruments and the same breathing machine I remember blowing into to practice taking inhalers as a kid. Not forgetting the different sized letters on the wall for eye tests.

Dad told the receptionist whilst booking the appointment that I had a tumour, so Dr. Evans was ready for the news, but I still don't think he believed it. However,

I wasn't going to leave the chair because I had a letter from the Copa Dor Hospital in my hand. There was one problem though – it was all written in Portuguese. Apart from the word 'tumour', of course.

Dr. Evans turned to his computer, pushed his glasses to the top of his nose, rolled his sleeves up to his elbows and slowly typed the letter into Google Translate. As the letter translated line by line his face started to drop further. I was sitting to the side of him and saw him take a gulp which made his Adam's apple move into his mouth and back down his throat. He wouldn't be prescribing paracetamol for this one.

He turned back to us, touched my knee and then looked into my eyes exactly how the doctor in Rio had done.

'Ok, it does look like they want to do more tests on a nodule, but I'm sure you'll be fine.' He held up the Portuguese letter. 'You have two options from here. I can refer you to a consultant and you'll get an appointment in about two weeks.'

I thought, *That's a crap option. I've got a letter here saying I have a tumour for Christ's sake. What's next? A Subway sandwich and a cup of tea?*

'Or I can refer you to a private clinic and a consultant can see you this afternoon, but it will cost you about six hundred pounds.' Dr. Evans turned to Dad.

Well, who would have thought it? Take my money. Take it all. Well, actually I don't have any money left but Dad will pay. Take Dad's money.

'Of course, we will pay anything to get this sorted as soon as possible,' Dad replied with a frog in his throat.

Go easy Dad we don't want to seem desperate and over price ourselves just yet, I thought.

Dr. Evans picked up the phone and made the appointment at the private clinic. So rather than wait two weeks, we paid the six hundred pounds and were going to see a consultant an hour later. It's a funny old game.

So off we went to Winterbourne Hospital, about a thirty-minute drive away, to the private appointment with a consultant. It must have been the tenth doctor or consultant in as many days and I was going to have to repeat the same story to him about how I found the tumour. I should've voice recorded it so I could play it each time I saw a new medical professional.

Dr. Andrews didn't do any tests at all. His office and bed were modern and gleaming. Radiant blue colours and modern lights to brighten the room. *This is the sort of doctor's room I deserve*, I thought. Six hundred pounds worth. He got me to lay on his office bed and pull my trousers and boxers down to my ankles. He had a good feel of my balls. I mean a REALLY good feel. It was intense, especially as Dad was just the other side of the paper-thin blue curtain that wrapped around me and the doc. Have you ever had another man feel your balls whilst your dad listened? This was a proper rummage.

It got a bit weird when he gave them a gentle squeeze and looked deeply into my eyes for a reaction, but the grope was conclusive. He instructed me to pull up my pants and take a seat at his desk next to Dad.

Dr. Andrews said directly and with intention, 'It looks like a tumour and it definitely feels like a tumour. Now you have two options.'

Ahh fucking great, the options game again. So far, my options had been gonorrhoea or a tumour, paying fifteen hundred pounds or choosing free surgery to remove a ball, and waiting two weeks for an appointment or paying six hundred pounds for a same day one. *So… what you got for me, Doc?*

'Option one is I refer you to a radiologist for an ultra-sound, but it will take about two weeks for a referral.'

Right. Ok, Doc, I've got a letter saying I have a tumour and you've just felt my balls for over five minutes and did your best Louis Walsh impression while judging the testicle factor: 'I tink it's amazing, it looks like a tumour, it feels like a tumour… I… want… you… in… surgery.'

Let me guess, does option two involve money?

'Or you can pay to go private and see the radiologist this afternoon. He has an available appointment in thirty minutes.' He then said that it would cost six hundred pounds but once I was in the system and had a diagnosis then everything else would be sped up and the NHS takes care of the rest for free.

'Do you take Mastercard?' Dad couldn't get his wallet out quick enough. He was like some sort of credit card wielding superhero. Is it a bird? Is it a plane? No, it's 'Mastercard Man', draped in an orange and red cape wearing a matching orange and red Zorro mask. Dad the credit card superhero would not be defeated this month by his arch nemesis *Interest Fees* and his kryptonite of *making monthly payments*. Booking a private consultation = six hundred pound. Seeing a consultant to get a cancer check in thirty minutes = priceless. Mastercard Man.

I felt sad that the system didn't allow everyone to do this. If I'd waited two weeks to see this consultant and then another two weeks for the radiologist, that would have been four weeks before getting close to a diagnosis. At the rate I was receiving news by the day, anything could happen in four weeks, and that didn't include the overthinking, worrying and stress for an added month. Dad wasn't exactly rich, but he'd face that financial problem when he came to it.

Dad gave Dr. Andrews the same look he gave my school geography teacher Mr Collins. There was no reduction in the six hundred pound fee, but we could pay it off in fifty pound monthly instalments. *Great, I'll be paying fifty pound a month for the next year for an intrusive rub of my balls. Still, that's cheaper than some London prices, so I've heard.*

Before Dr. Andrews gave us the chance to leave, he whipped out what looked like a brown mahogany cigar box. I usually associate cigars with a celebration but I wasn't sure this was the right time. *Was this included in the six hundred pounds – a fondle, a diagnosis and a celebratory cigar? Still, cheaper than some London prices.* The doctor opened the cigar-like box to reveal eight different shaped transparent silicone balls. He took one of the balls out of the box that looked a similar size to my healthy testicle that he'd just felt.

'If you have your testicle removed, which I think is likely, then you have the option to get an implant to replace it.' Dad and I looked at each other like it was a new world. Dad was used to seeing silicone and fake boobs in his nightclub and now his son was being offered a fake silicone testicle. The doctor gave me the silicone ball to have a feel. It felt light. My first thoughts were, *Will it float in the bath? I wonder if they do ones that light up.*

'Getting an artificial testicle is purely for aesthetics. Some men like to have two down there, but it will take longer to heal and brings a higher risk of infection. If you require further treatment then the fake ball might delay you getting this. You can always have one fitted at a later date,' the doc told us with no sense of absurdity in his voice. I guess it was usual practice for him.

But for me, I had only gone in for a diagnosis that morning and now I was looking at what size fake testicle I could get to make my ball bag more pleasing on the eye. *Maybe I could get a huge one for a laugh*, I thought. I'm not sure I would ever look at a ball bag and think, *Do you know what? This ugly ball bag really needs another ball inside it.* A scrotum is a scrotum and that's that.

I decided it wasn't the time for more delays, no matter how aesthetically pleasing they may be, so I declined the offer and the doctor put away his cigar box of fake testes and made a phone call to a radiologist at a nearby hospital.

Dad and I were soon driving as fast as we could to Dorset County Hospital in Dorchester, a further ten minutes away. The windows were down, and the cold air was blowing in, but at least the smell of Marlboro cigarettes was fading. Mum was also driving from Weymouth to meet us, so I called her to let her know we were now travelling to Dorset County Hospital radiology department instead.

After sitting in the waiting room, Dad and I were called for the ultrasound by a man with shaggy hair. Not as shaggy as Brazilian Dr. Shaggy; this man's was Liam Gallagher-esque. He was even wearing his lab coat like a parka jacket. Maybe the hairdo is one of the prerequisites for a job as an ultrasound sonographer.

Dad waited outside for me as I knew what this procedure entailed, and he didn't need to see me with my pants round my ankles for the second time today. The Liam Gallagher sonographer applied the blue gel to my testicles, giving me a cold jolting sensation. There is no amount of bracing yourself that will ever stop that body-shuddering reaction. He started scanning the healthy right testicle, I guess for a reference point. Then he moved over to the left little son of a bitch Evil Jose. They looked exactly the same. I swear they really did.

Afterwards, I pulled up my pants and waited to see if we would hug it out like Brazilian Dr. Shaggy. I was ready for it this time.

But all he said was, 'Take a seat in the waiting room and I'll call you through shortly.'

I left the room and took a seat opposite Dad.

'What did he say then?' Dad asked, expecting to know all of the answers straight away.

'He said wait.'

After a long five minutes, the sonographer returned and asked us into his office. Inside, it was pitch black apart from his lit-up computer screen with images of my testicles on it.

'I'm afraid it's cancer.'

Oohhhh fuck. Straight in with it. He's actually said the C word. No one up to this point had said 'cancer'. *What happened to the nodule and the tumour? Fucking cancer. What!* Over ten doctors, consultants and specialists across two continents hadn't mentioned the word cancer. Dad shrunk from five-foot-three to three-foot-three, and I sat on the edge of the chair and puffed my chest out.

'So, what now?' I asked.

'We'll need to do an orchidectomy – a removal of the testicle – this week, and then after some tests we'll put you on a course of chemotherapy.'

Wohhhh chemotherapy? Stop with the devastating C words, man. I was barely ready for cancer and now you're throwing chemo at me as well. I'm going to lose an entire fucking ball. I thought maybe just cut the bad part out. And what happens to my ball? Does it just go away? Questions, questions, questions. Give me answers.

'What sort of chemotherapy? Will I lose my hair?'

'Until we do tests on the testicle, we won't be able to tell but it's aggressive enough.'

Aggressive? Another harsh word, man. Say benign or malignant, don't call it aggressive. No wonder it felt like people were passing the buck with me.

'Oh, and you said you first noticed the problem because your back was hurting?'

'Yes, why's that?' I put my hand onto my back where it had hurt.

'Well… we'll need to do a CT scan on your body to see if the cancer has spread.' *SPREAD! Come again? A CT scan? It's spread?*

Dad was now one foot nothing and shrinking into the ground like a little Iranian borrower.

'I'll refer you for surgery and a CT scan this week and then you'll be sent a chemotherapy schedule which will take place at Southampton Hospital. I'd say as chemo goes it's probably about two thirds up the scale as bad as chemo you can have.'

This was the most honest Liam Gallagher sonographer lookalike I'd ever met. As he finished his gig to me and Dad, I almost expected him to put both his hands behind his back, tilt his head into his stethoscope as a pretend microphone and shout, 'Thank you, Dorchester!' before walking off.

Dad and I left the building and headed back to the car. I couldn't believe it.

I've got cancer! CANCER! I'm twenty-nine and I've got cancer. I'm going to have chemo. Am I going to lose my hair? What a fucking day this has turned out to be.

I was plodding across the hospital car park, Dad shuffling along behind me dragging his heels and sucking on an E-cigarette, when Mum appeared, walking briskly towards us. She was looking excited at the fact we'd gone in and out of the appointment before she'd even had time to arrive.

With hope in her voice, she asked, 'So, is it good news?'

8. Welcome To The Club

Life Lesson: There are five stages of grief.
Cancer Lesson: Find a cancer buddy.
Song Choice: *You've Got a Friend in Me* – Randy Newman

As your cancer diagnosis sinks in, it might cross your mind to start telling friends and family about your latest news. Again, I say 'might' because not everyone does. Everyone reacts differently, but one day, when no one has seen you for three weeks and you bump into someone with your new bald head, it will raise suspicions. It's not the news you might go Facebook Live with or post on to your Instagram story, but sharing what's happening with close friends and family is a good starting point.

News travels fast and the world begins to rush past in every sense. It's still just words and emotions though, right? You probably won't feel physically different right away. You know cancer is terrible, but how terrible? When you hear the word cancer, you might instantly think cancer = death. And so might other people. And their reactions can be eye-opening and, at times, humorous.

When I became aware of this pattern of responses, it was sometimes quite amusing. The classic five stages of grief are generally agreed to be:

- Denial,
- Anger,
- Bargaining,
- Depression,

- Acceptance.

There's a famous episode of *The Simpsons* where Homer eats a poisonous blowfish and has twenty-four hours to live. Doctor Hibbert tells Homer about the five stages of grief, and he goes through the emotions as quickly as each sentence is finished. It's a fantastic scene and you should YouTube it. It'll make sense of what happens when you deliver your own news to people. I called John, my best friend in Essex, and he went through the five stages of grief within one phone call.

'They've confirmed I've got cancer.'

There was silence on the other side of the phone as the realisation hit John.

'No, you haven't. Ask to get another test.'

'I've had about four tests now, John.'

'Why didn't they tell you after the first test? This isn't right. Whose fault is this?'

'Well, I was on the other side of the world, but it's fine, they were just doing their job.'

'I feel helpless, I live too far away, I can't do anything.'

'It's ok, mate. No one needs to do anything right now.'

'I'm going to raise money for you. I'll walk from Essex to Weymouth. I'll walk it in my bare feet.'

'Mate, it's fine, just chill.'

'Ok, you're right, we're gonna fucking beat this shit.'

John moved from stage one denial to stage five acceptance in less than a minute. The walking barefoot to my house was a bit extreme, but he got through the stages quicker than most. Especially compared to other friends and family around me.

It's important to note the five stages are not linear, and you can continue to fleet between them. You can be at acceptance one day and then fall back into denial the next. And so can other people.

As well as John's reaction, there were brilliantly comical phone conversations, like one with Paul, an old work colleague. Paul had noticed I was back in the UK, so randomly phoned me for a chat.

'Why you back then? Run out of money?'

'Not just yet. I went to the doctors in Rio and they said it was best to fly home.'

'Sounds bad, was it another outbreak of chlamydia?' He burst out laughing.

'No, they found a tumour, and I've just been told it's cancer.'

'Ahh… I bet you wish it was chlamydia then.'

Luckily, we both broke into fits of laughter, but I preferred that reaction to people welling up and crying.

Cancer treatment and managing your emotions are all measurable and in certain ways, within your control. What isn't in your control are the emotions of the people around you. When people feel helpless, they can become even more upset than usual. This, you don't need.

After Dr Liam Gallagher told us it was cancer, Mum and I left Dorset County Hospital and sat silently for the twenty-minute drive home. I pulled out my phone and sent a message to a WhatsApp group called Bantz, with my school friends George, Dave and Rich in it.

Lads, they just confirmed it... I've got cancer!

Ahhh, bollocks, Dave typed. I was unsure if he was trying to be ironic or not.

So, are we going out this weekend or not? George added the denial.

Are we still playing badminton tonight? Rich was being deadly serious.

I love the lads and I don't know if they felt their role was to 'keep it real' or to keep me grounded, or maybe they couldn't process what I was saying. Not even I knew how to react. But it did make me laugh, much to Mum's annoyance.

I got home to Mum's house, laid on the bed, and looked up at the ceiling for answers. I wanted to speak to someone who'd been in the same situation. I sent a message to the only person I knew who'd had cancer. A lad about town called Julian Quick.

Julian was captain of the Weymouth rugby team and a mountain of a man in stature and personality. We knew each other from drunken nights out. He's over six feet tall and always messing around with people and making jokes like I do. Everybody knows who Julian is, he is Mr Weymouth. The last time I'd seen him, we were both standing at a bar, and he'd tapped a girl's shoulder in front of me. She turned around and pushed me thinking it was me. Julian pointed at me, roared with laughter and shouted, 'Wayyy.' That's Julian, the life and soul of every party, and he's usually dancing with his top off at some point during the night.

I went to Facebook messenger, opened up my inbox to Julian, and read the only two previous conversations we'd had on the chat.

The first conversation was four years earlier.

29th April 2012 – Facebook Messenger:
Julian: *Hey babes, so are we walking up the big K? x*
Af: *Big time, two grand. Christmas time, summit new year's day. Have you got the balls? x*

It was ironic that I'd called him out for having balls when I was now days away from losing one of mine. The night before these messages we'd been massively drunk and egging each other on to climb Mount Kilimanjaro. The idea had fizzled out along with our hangovers. We weren't really anything more than enthusiastic ramblers when it came to mountains, but I'd done some trekking in Nepal, and Julian had conquered Mont Blanc.

The second conversation was three years later, on 27th December 2015. Again, it was the morning after the night before, but I hadn't recognised him. It wasn't until the next day that Rich told me it was Julian who had been sitting at a table in Dad's bar. He had looked completely different; very thin, not giant anymore, and he'd had patches of hair on his head. I hadn't known, but he'd been undergoing chemotherapy for a rare bone cancer called Ewing's Sarcoma.

27th December 2015 – Facebook Messenger:
Af: *Yo dude, I don't know if I've been living under a rock or what, but I've only just seen your Facebook, blogs and*

shit news about your year. Sorry to hear about it all and massive apologies I haven't been in touch. Hope things are looking up buddy. Maybe we can still walk up that mountain one day, but by the looks of it, you have already conquered the tallest one. All the best mate.

Julian: *Hey mate! Was meant to come and say hi last night. Thanks for the message, and I'm always up for any challenge.*

Af: *You call it, you play it. Let's do it.*

I didn't know anyone else who'd had cancer. Certainly not around my age anyway, so I thought maybe Julian could give me some advice, any advice whatsoever. Everyone around me was either in denial, angry, or crumbling like a flaky pastry, so I messaged him…

13th September 2016 – Facebook Messenger:

Af: *Yo Julian, you there?*

Julian: *Hello mate, yes just getting ready. How are you? I've been enjoying your behind-the-scenes videos from Rio.*

Af: *I was just wondering if I could have a bit of a chat with you. Rio was going tremendous, but got that news no one wants yesterday. I went to a hospital in Rio Thursday, they found a tumour, flew home Friday. Got testicular cancer, had all the scans and got a CT scan tomorrow to see if it's spread.*

Julian: *I am so sorry to hear that. Welcome to the club.*

Af: *Haha, thanks. Is it an actual club? Hope you don't mind me telling you this, just you're one of the people I know that have gone through it.*

Julian: *I know exactly how you feel mate. Absolutely anything you want to ask, any time of day or night, I'm here.*

Julian and I spoke on messenger about everything I had on my mind. There weren't many medical questions. We talked more about emotions. I told him I hadn't gotten that upset, yet everyone around me was losing control. Everyone was crying but me. He'd been through the same. I asked what other emotional bombshells I should expect along the journey.

Julian: *There are no rules. You cry whenever you want to cry. Life gets very different and my life will never feel the same, but it doesn't hit you all at once. Your mates and family will all be around you, some old friends will come out of the woodwork, and you might realise some close friends aren't actually that close.*

So, there it was, the most real chat I'd had with anyone in ten days. No one was crying, no one was ignoring it, no one was trying to be overly pragmatic and calm. It was just genuine. Even the doctors who work in the environment every day were struggling to be honest or give me reassurance. It was an eye-opener that Julian was being so direct about it all.
Welcome to the club. He wished me good luck at the doctor's and gave me his mobile number.

Julian: *If you ever need any advice or just a chat, then text or call that number as it's a dedicated support line to the world's sexiest nurse. Let me know how it goes at the doctor's and let's get a coffee sometime.*

Hero!

9.   The CT Scan

Life Lesson: CT scans heighten radiation risks.
Cancer Lesson: Have a late dinner the night before a CT scan.
Song Choice: *Good Morning* – Kanye West

Most cancers have four stages. Some cancers are classified as Stage 0, or in situ where the abnormal cells have the potential to develop into cancer. Stage one cancer is usually when cancerous cells are in one location like a testicle or a breast. Stage two is if the cancer progresses and spreads to nearby lymph nodes. Stage three the cancer has spread to distant organs such as the lungs, liver, or bones, and stage four is when it reaches the brain. So yes, testicular cancer can spread to the brain and still be referred to as testicular cancer. Testicular cancer is typically staged using the TNM system, which considers the tumour's size and extent, lymph node involvement, and the presence of distant metastasis (Macmillan).

The first tests to analyse suspected testicular cancer usually begins with an ultrasound of the testicles and a blood test. Depending on the results, further scans, like a CT scan, may be required to assess the extent of the problem. This is when *scanxiety* comes into play. A fear of scans. Or the fear of what news they may bring at least. It becomes a common thing for people going through cancer and also those in remission.

After Monday's confirmation from the radiologist Dr Liam Gallagher that I had testicular cancer, I needed to return to Dorset County Hospital on Tuesday morning for a CT Scan. I'd never had a CT scan, but they sounded like serious business. You aren't allowed to eat or drink for at least eight hours before a scan. This wouldn't have been an issue, but I'd had an early dinner the night before and hadn't eaten all morning. By the time of my appointment, I was starving.

A CT scan processes multiple X-Rays to produce tomograph images of inside the body without cutting you open. It can show bone, joint, or organ problems. It can show internal bleeding or detect tumours. It's what they need on the *Great British Bake Off* to see inside the cake without having to slice it. However, slicing it does mean more cake. Hmm, lovely cake.

The CT scan is a vital diagnosis process to show where a tumour is and measure how big it is. You can't have them too regularly though because of the radiation levels they give off. So, when you go for one, make sure you're ready.

Dad drove us to Dorset County Hospital and as soon as we arrived, a nurse called me through to take my observations. Observations or 'obs' usually consist of taking your pulse, blood pressure, temperature, those sorts of things. As a cancer patient, you go to the front of all the queues, and waiting time is very short. *Move out the way small boy with a broken arm, I'm coming straight through.*

'What's your full name and date of birth?' the nurse asked, checking if I was the right patient for the scan. *Who would possibly want to steal my identity at this moment in time?* I thought. I followed the nurse down the corridor and into the radiology room, The door was covered in yellow caution and red danger radiation warning signs. Above it was a sign that lit up red with the word OCCUPIED, just like a radio DJ's 'on air' signal. I was going 'live in the studio'.

The nurse talked me through the procedure: she'd put a cannula into my arm that would pump dye into my body and I'd lay down on a long stretcher, that moved into a circular contraption. It looked like it led to a Stargate dimension. First though, I had to go behind a curtain, remove my clothes and jewellery to make sure I had no metal on me. I swapped my clothes for a thin blue gown that didn't quite tie up at the back, leaving a fresh draught.

As I returned to the main radiology room, the nurse was waiting with a tourniquet to wrap around my bicep. She asked me to clench my fist to get the blood flowing to my arm so my veins would show. After a few attempts of not being able to find a juicy vein to insert the needle into, she repeated the procedure on my other arm, tapping my veins to entice them to the surface like a heroin addict. Once she'd got the cannula in, she gave me a set of headphones and took her position sitting behind a glass box in the corner of the room. *Why's she all the way over there?* I wondered. Shielded and protected from high radiation levels, that's why.

I laid down on the stretcher and shut my eyes tightly, imagining I was back on a sun lounger in Rio with Luci beside me, telling me to relax. The nurse spoke to me through the headphones and instructed me to move my hands behind my head. I nervously moved my arms above me in fear that one false move would rip the cannula out of my arm and cause blood to spurt out. It was as if I was a scientific experiment. We were now in full air traffic control mode, and she spoke to me as if we were in NASA and I was the trainee astronaut.

The stretcher started to move slowly towards the circular dimension, and I opened my eyes, noticing that the giant CT scanning machine was manufactured by Samsung. My mind drifted off. *Is Samsung a mobile phone company that makes CT scanners or are they a CT scanner manufacturer that makes mobile phones? I'll have to google that when I get out of this. Stop thinking about Samsung, Af... focus.*

And then I heard a female computer voice start talking to me through the headphones.

'Breathe in... hold.' The stretcher slowly exited the scanner to its original position and the godlike voice spoke again.

'And breathe out.'

That seemed easy enough.

The stretcher started moving back into the cubicle.

'Breathe in... hold... and breathe out.'

This happened over and over again, and with each scan something slightly different happened, and a louder noise occurred. At one point, the machine got so loud it felt like it was about to take off and I wondered if maybe this time it would actually transport me back in time like the DeLorean. Yes, take me back to three months ago, please.

The scanner rolled me into the device for the fifth or sixth time and suddenly, my body got hotter. It felt like the cannula had become unattached and that the dye that was being pumped into me was dripping over my arm. The same warm sensation moved up to my shoulders, through my neck, into my mouth and finished at the top of my head. I could literally taste the dye in my mouth. The dye started moving back down my body to my bladder. That same feeling of the dye dripping was now happening through my entire crotch. I didn't know if the heat in my head was from the dye or if I was having a hot flush and pissing everywhere in the Samsung DeLorean space machine.

As the machine finally stopped and the stretcher moved out, the nurse told me that I could sit up again and change back into my clothes. I sat up slowly and looked down at my crotch, but it was completely dry. I patted down my pants and down my legs and couldn't believe I hadn't pissed myself. I got dressed back into my clothes, and the nurse of the Starship enterprise asked me to wait in the waiting room for ten minutes in case I came out with a rash. Any rash would show an allergic reaction to the dye and I'd have to be rushed to A&E immediately.

I drank three cups of water and looked down at my arm. I now had a patch of hair missing from where the cannula had been inserted. *I can't keep having these cannulas with my hairy hands and arms. Ripping the surgical tape off is causing me some of the worst pain.* If the appointments, scans and cannulas weren't enough to deal with, it felt like each appointment always finished with a waxing session. *If the cannulas are hurting this much, then how bad will the rest of this shit be?* My challenges in Rio involved climbing mountains, finding new apartments to stay in and wondering where my next job and life would take me. Those were the challenges I wanted. Not this.

Dr Liam Gallagher called us into his darkened room again and showed us the images on his computer screen.

'So, Afsheen, the tumour has travelled to your lymph nodes. You will require chemotherapy to get rid of this.'

What the fuck is a lymph node? I didn't feel shocked anymore, or sad. Just numb.

'Ok, what stage cancer do I have?' I replied and saw Dad shudder as I said the word cancer.

'It's stage two. You'll have to see a specialist in Southampton for your chemotherapy schedule, bank sperm before if you'd like children one day, and you'll lose your hair around the third week of chemotherapy.'

Now I was nervous. What else was this going to throw at me? I flew home on Saturday from the trip of a lifetime and seventy-two hours later I had stage two cancer and needed to think about my future children. Everyone had been telling me not to worry. Everyone! Well, I was starting to fucking worry. *I won't be listening to anyone who keeps telling me not to worry. This is my body and I know it more than anyone else.*

Dad and I got back into the car to drive home to Weymouth. We sat in silence and I glanced across to see Dad's frowned facial expression.

'I can't believe this is happening.' Dad gripped the steering wheel firmly with both hands.

'Yeah, it's hard to take in,' I half-heartedly replied. I felt guilty for causing him so much worry but it wasn't as if I was doing this on purpose.

'Honestly, Afsheen, this is the worst thing that's ever happened to me.' Dad stared intently down the road.

To him? The worst thing that's ever happened to him? What about me?

10.   You Got This

Life Lesson: No one achieved anything without the support of others.
Cancer Lesson: You got this.
Song Choice: *Seven Days* – Craig David

So, you've told your family and they're dealing with it in ways you couldn't have imagined. You've told your close friends and they've either decided to start crying, ignore it or laugh it off as some humorous joke. Now there's a choice you have to make, and I would listen to your own gut on this one.

I have always posted on Facebook, Twitter and Instagram, and written the occasional blog from time to time. Portraying your life on social media can have its positives AND its negatives as to how people perceive you. Before cancer, I posted on Facebook about life, travelling and adventures and received replies from people saying I had made them laugh or inspired them. On the other hand, I have also been told I was attention seeking and posting publicly to get 'likes' to fill my void. That was a bit harsh, but that's social media for you.

A friend once told me they thought I always posted my life for likes, but after ten years of adventures, they said to themselves, 'Maybe he actually likes going on adventures.' Imagine thinking I'd flown all the way to Nepal and trekked to 14,000 feet just for 156 likes on a photo. Either way, if you post on social media, you'll be judged. It can be truly amazing but it can also be toxic.

The thing about cancer is that it is a challenge. One of the biggest you can face. If you've ever done a challenge, then you'll know how you personally prepare for it. If you've run a marathon, half-marathon, or a 5k race, you'll have probably asked for advice from people that have run before. They might tell you to take a drink, eat the right food, buy suitable trainers, and maybe even post about it on social media, for extra motivation. So, you should use the same principle in preparation for cancer. Would you climb a mountain without asking anyone how to climb a mountain? Would you do it without walking boots? If the answer to these questions is yes, then you're just making things more difficult for yourself. Treat it like another challenge, but with more dedication than you've ever had before.

If you decide not to post on social media about your cancer challenge, I would suggest joining some social media pages and cancer communities. I've met some very good online friends through these. If you search for your cancer on somewhere like Facebook, then you're bound to find a support group for it. I wish it was mentioned to me sooner in my diagnosis as groups like Testicular Cancer UK (formally Checkemlads), Cancer Lads, and The Cancer Club have been a real asset to men in terms of supporting each other and asking questions of uncertainty.

There are also charities for all types of cancer and age brackets. Trekstock is a fantastic UK charity that offers tailored support to young adults going through cancer in their twenties and thirties. They provide a range of support, workshops and in-person meetups. Trekstock have some amazing post-cancer offers and opportunities too. You'll know what type of person you are and whether you think your challenge is worth sharing, but my story might give you an idea of what it's like.

As Craig David pointed out, a lot can happen in seven days. However, my last week had been a slightly tragic remixed rendition of his hit song.

Got diagnosed with cancer on Monday, had a CT scan on Tuesday, had an operation on Thursday, recovered on Friday and Saturday, chilled on Sunday.

Within five days, I'd flown home from Brazil, told my family I had a tumour, got diagnosed with testicular cancer, had a scan, learned it had spread, and now had an operation scheduled for Thursday. As far as weeks go, it was quite the fall from grace.

On Wednesday, the night before my operation, I was speaking with Rich on the phone about how I should tell people.

'Do you think I wait until the evening to do a post or not post anything at all?'

'You post shit if you're eating a kebab on a Saturday night, so just do what you normally do.'

I'd always posted on social media ever since Facebook was invented in my first year of university. It was a great way to upload photos and stay in touch with friends. Then, after living and working in Essex, it was always good to keep in contact with people and post about the adventures and challenges I was up to.

I sat in my bedroom with my laptop on my knees and wrote a Facebook status. After posting the status, I shut the laptop. I left it with my phone on the bed and went downstairs to watch TV with Mum for the rest of the evening to switch off.

5:40pm on 14th September 2016 – Facebook:

Af's next challenge – cancer!
Yep, you read that correctly.
I found out Monday that I have cancer and I start treatment tomorrow.
'Fuck!' Yeah, that's what I said too.
'Shit!' Yeah, I said that as well.
After thinking I had an infection last Thursday, I went to a hospital in Rio de Janeiro to ask for some antibiotics as I was flying to Argentina the next day to start my travelling adventure in South America.
After some tests and scans I was told that I had a tumour.
I flew back to England the next day and landed at Heathrow on Saturday afternoon.
On Monday, I saw a consultant and then had an ultrasound and a CT scan, which confirmed it.
Unfortunately, the primary cancer has spread to a secondary place in my body.
Tomorrow morning, I have surgery in Dorset County Hospital to cut out the first bit of the big C, and then I'm hoping to start chemotherapy next week to zap the rest.
I know this is a bit of a shock and is making people sad, but team, we got this. My family and friends have been brilliant, and I know they will continue to support me and make me laugh along the way.
Last week I was climbing mountains in Brazil and now I

am about to start climbing my next mountain, just a different kind.

Tomorrow I will be in surgery and I'm hoping I'll wake up in time to watch Southampton play Sparta Prague in the Europa League. If I am not, I'll watch the highlights so please don't anyone tell me the scores.

I've always been a firm believer that everything happens for a reason and this is just another one of those life challenges that we will complete together. So far, I've been positive most of the time and I intend to keep it that way. I'm sure I'll have down days.

Someone asked me after the Olympics, 'What was your summer experience like on a scale of 1-10?'

I said instantly, 'A ten of course.' But then I said, 'Every day is a ten no matter what I'm doing. We're living, aren't we? What a time to be alive!'

Ok, maybe being told I had cancer was about a 7 out of 10 day, but still.

So… I'm going on an adventure and you're all invited to come on this one with me. If you don't think you can do anything to help, then you'll be surprised of the power of a simple text. You never know what's around the corner and life is the most precious and glorious thing. So if there's anything to come out of this post and my experience, go make sure you tell someone that you love them tonight!

Lots of Love, Afsheen

What a time to be alive!!!!!!!!!

I got back to my bedroom just after 9pm and picked up my phone to see my Facebook notifications had gone wild: four hundred and twenty five reactions, three hundred and twenty two comments, fourteen shares and forty inbox messages.

My phone had fifty two missed calls and over one hundred text messages and WhatsApps.

I wasn't expecting the response I had from everyone. I wasn't exactly smiling at my phone at how many 'likes' I was getting. This isn't what I wanted likes for; it was making people sad. There were some truly amazing words and I thought to myself, *Why has it taken cancer for them to tell me what they really think of me?*

As I was reading some of the comments, an old football team mate phoned me.

'Is your status serious? You can't joke about stuff like that,' he said, without even saying hello.

'Yeah, unfortunately it is, mate.'

He got emotional and told me that I was too young and that his mum had just died of cancer.

Many people had said that my lifestyle and outlook on life had inspired them, but no one had ever told me. It was nice to hear but honestly, I just wanted to talk to Rich, Dave and George about tomorrow's football fixtures.

There was one message that I noticed kept repeating as I was reading through the comments: *You got this, Af* and *If anyone's got this, Af, it's you.* One message after the other. *Af, you got this, buddy. You got this.* I didn't really know what to say to people. A lot of people were taking it seriously, way more seriously than I was.

Even though the responses were vast and overwhelming, now that I'd told the world, it felt like a lot was off my chest and no longer weighing me down. It was only cancer. I've run marathons, cycled long distances and climbed mountains.

Surely it can't be that hard, can it?

11. Operation

Life Lesson: You only get one mum.
Cancer Lesson: You're pregnant.
Song Choice: *Don't Go Breaking My Heart* – Elton John and Kiki Dee

Operation day! It was an early wake-up after a restless night's sleep. The kind of broken sleep you have before a 6am budget flight to southern Spain that you only booked because it was just £29 with hand luggage. A day that needs to start with eating a hearty breakfast. The kind of early morning breakfast you have before an all-day drinking session because you know you won't be eating again and need to line your stomach. It's the airport pre-flight full-English breakfast, usually coupled with a beer to wash down the over-priced excuse of a sausage, which has the taste of knowing that soon you'll be poolside drinking pina coladas at the all-inclusive bar.

But in this case… it's the anticipation of not having a testicle with a malignant tumour inside you by the end of the day. It's bittersweet really. You're about to lose half of your crown jewels, but… there's no more tumour. Just like the overpriced and unnecessary airport beer, it's a price you're willing to pay. It's just a routine operation so I'm not sure there is much to fear, especially as you'll be asleep for it anyway.

If you're about to go through it, just make sure the people around you are prepared for the aftermath and recovery too.

I still hadn't searched online for anything about tumours, cancers or operations. Maybe I should have, but I didn't want to scare myself even more by asking Dr. Google. I hadn't thought about the operation, how long it would last or how painful it would be. I just continued to remain as normal as possible.

On that Thursday – operation day – my football team Southampton were playing in Europe for the first time in my lifetime. I spent the morning texting the lads about our chances against Sparta Prague. I knew this was a big day because for some reason Mum, Dad, AND my sister came to the hospital with me. It was the first time the four of us had done something together since Mum and Dad had divorced. What an occasion for a family reunion.

My sister, Nas, is the pragmatic one of the family, always offering practical solutions before emotions. She is five years older than me and has always been a huge influence on my decision-making and the paths I've taken. Nas arrived at the hospital and the nurse welcomed her in by saying, 'Ahh your wife is here.' An easy mistake to make as we have the same surname, but look nothing like siblings. She has Mum's fair skin and hair but Dad's curly locks, which are styled down to her shoulders.

The consultant called Mum, Nas and me into his office, as Dad was outside having another crafty cigarette off the hospital site. The consultant, Dr Amafoa, had a strong Ghanaian accent.

'Good morning all. How are you feeling today, Mr Afsheen?' Dr Amafoa sat back in his chair, with his hands resting on his belly and fingers intertwined.

'Bit nervous to be honest,' I admitted.

'Ok, well, your tests have come back. They are positive and you're pregnant.'

'Huh?'

'Your pregnancy test came back positive!'

I looked to my left at Mum, she looked across me to Nas and we all looked back to Dr Amafoa with three confused faces. *I'm all for jokes and good humour, Doc, but I've just admitted for the first time that I'm scared and you're coming out with a joke that I'm pregnant with hours left until I'm about to lose a bollock*, I thought.

Nas's logical thinking kicked into action.

'Would that be the HCG hormone?' Nas sat forward like a journalist asking questions at a press conference.

'Yes, Mr Afsheen's HCG hormone levels are very high.' Dr Amafoa was showing little clarity, like a football manager holding onto his latest transfer news.

I looked at Nas a bit concerned with the face that said, *Do I want this man operating on me?*

Nas told Mum about the HCG hormone like she was explaining a foreign language.

'If a man has testicular cancer, then they are over producing the HCG hormone, which is the same hormone pregnant women produce. So, if you were to wee on a pregnancy stick then it will show positive,' Nas explained while Dr Amafoa sat nodding along as he reclined further back in his chair. It's not exactly the most accurate test, but it's true that if you have testicular cancer and pee on a pregnancy stick, it will test positive.

'This all sounds conclusive,' I jokingly replied.

'Don't worry, Mr Afsheen. If you had to choose to have any cancer, then this would be the one.'

If I had to choose a cancer? This guy's fucking mental.

Thank goodness for Nas's pragmatic and rational thinking. If she wasn't panicking, then neither was I, even though this doctor was coming out with the most random conversation.

I shook off the confusion and got changed into a surgical gown. Before heading back to the waiting room, Dr Amafoa explained to us about the surgical procedure, or the 'orchidectomy' as it is medically known. You would think they would make an incision in your scrotum and remove the testicle from your ball bag. No, that's not the case as that has a risk of spreading cancerous cells. They cut you open just below your waistband and remove the testicle by pulling it up through your pubic area! When you're a tiny little foetus this is where boys testicles live before they descend. They then clamp the spermatic cord, cut it, and detach the testicle. How about that? The new detachable spermatic cordless ball. Sounds like a great selling point of the latest Dyson vacuum.

Mum, Dad and Nas were talking about who was going to take me home after surgery and whose house I could sleep at that night. I continued texting the lads and focussing on Southampton's potential starting line-up for the evening's Europa League game.

Dad suggested I should go back to his house because he'd made up a bed for me in the living room, next to his bay windows that overlook Weymouth. A very relaxing location.

But Mum wanted to take care of me. Mum had spent her life caring for people and putting others first. She worked as a residential nurse, she had raised two children as a single parent, and she cared for her horses. Her life came second, behind everyone else, and now I was sick she wanted to go full Mum mode and look after her 'good little boy' again. She wanted to be at my bedside spoon feeding me ladles of Calpol. But no amount of Calpol was going to make this go away, and since moving away at eighteen years old, maybe I wasn't 'mummy's little solider' anymore.

However, I've never slept at my dad's house in my life. He had his new family with his wife, Shohreh, and my younger brother, Parsa, who was eleven. So why would I stay there now?

But something didn't feel right. Since leaving home for university ten years ago, every time I returned to stay at Mum's house, I had to take an antihistamine to stop me from sneezing due to an allergy to horsehair. When I'd moved out, the dogs had moved into the lounge and onto my spot on the sofa. I always loved going back to Mum's house and sleeping in my childhood bedroom, but even that was cluttered with piles of stuff now. I couldn't come out of surgery and lie in my cluttered room for days or have to take antihistamines just to stop me from sneezing. Who knew what could happen – one big sneeze could be horrific and rip open a fresh surgical wound.

Dr Amafoa came out of his office again and crouched down in front of me in the waiting room. He asked me to lift my surgical gown above my thighs. He had a thick black marker pen in his hand.

'Which testicle is it again?' he said out the side of his mouth, as he now had the marker pen lid between his teeth like he was chewing on the end of a cigar.

'It's the left one,' I stated back with some conviction and pointing.

'Ahh yes, just checking.' He put his left hand on my left knee for balance, held the marker pen in his right hand, and in thick black capital letters wrote the word LEFT on the inside of my left thigh, with an arrow the size of my thigh bone pointing towards my testicle.

I stared at my new tattoo and for half a split-second thought, *Maybe I'll get the word LEFT and an arrow tattooed on my leg after all this as a poignant reminder to myself.* I now wasn't just worried about the fact I had cancer, or about the surgery, or that I was pregnant. I now wondered how many times Dr Amafoa had accidentally removed the wrong testicle from someone because he hadn't drawn an arrow on their leg. Or even worse, removed something other than a testicle because he'd drawn an arrow pointing the wrong way. What would've happened if he'd just written LEFT and no arrow? *Christ, this is all I need.*

'Don't worry, we're going to get this out of you.' Dr Amafoa double tapped my knee like all the doctors had done when they wanted to settle my nerves and left, back to his office. Just that one sentence made me believe him and I knew I was going to be ok.

Mum and Dad had both watched nervously, whilst Nas was outside returning some missed calls. For once in my life, my what to say and what not to say filter was turned off. With the word LEFT written on the inside of my thigh, I finally thought it was time to say out loud how I felt.

'I think I'm going to go back to Dad's house after this to recover there.' I quickly looked back at my phone to see if the lads had texted me anything funny to distract myself with.

'What? You can't do that, I've got everything ready for you at home. I've cleaned the living room and the dogs are staying in the back room.' Mum's eyes started to moisten.

'I'm sorry, Mum, but this isn't just a cold I'm dealing with. I need to be comfortable.'

'You will be comfortable; I'll make it more comfortable.'

'Mum, it's only a few days and then I'll be back, but I can't stay in bed sneezing.'

'But… but…' Mum started crying. Crying like I'd never seen before. Until then, the worst I'd ever seen Mum cry was when our dog died when I was twelve years old. But this was worse. She was hysterical, crying like I'd just told her she wasn't my mum anymore. Like I'd just fired her as my mum and handed her a P45. She'd spent her life care giving. This was her World Cup final, and I'd just put her on the subs bench. *Oh fuck, this isn't what I wanted to happen.* I was thirty minutes away from having a cancerous testicle removed and I didn't need extreme emotions, even if I had just broken Mum's heart.

I sat there with frustrated eyebrows and a clenched jaw, staring out the window and hoping everything would stop. I was the one having part of my anatomy removed, I was the one with cancer.

Mum stormed out of the ward crying, and I knew she was going to find Nas to complain about me. Nas would probably have a go at me in her 'disappointed, not angry' tone of voice.

I sat there in my surgical gown on a black plastic chair waiting to be called to the operating theatre. Surely being in theatre would be better than being here. I continued staring out of the window because I knew I'd upset Mum, even though it was only going to be for a few days.

Dad sat next to me tensely in silence, with a finger and thumb either side of the outline of a cigarette box in his pocket, holding it with anxiety until he could go and find another smoky corner.

Well, this is all very shit. Inject me with the strongest anaesthetic right now and send me to fucking sleep...

12.   Post Op – Ignorance Is Bliss

Life Lesson: Your body will change.
Cancer Lesson: Operations can cause constipation.
Song Choice: *Boys Will Be Boys* – The Ordinary Boys

Those anaesthetic drugs are a knockout. I was waiting on a bed before surgery and a male nurse collected me and pushed me through to the operating theatre. He asked me what I thought Southampton's starting line-up should be in that night's Europa League game against Sparta Prague and by the time I'd finished saying, 'Virgil Van Dijk', I was asleep.

I was so dazed when I woke up that I asked a different, older, female nurse how many teeth they'd just removed. My head was in fairyland on drugs, so god knows what else I was saying. I looked up at a huge clock on the wall thinking it must be the evening, but it was only forty-five minutes since I had entered the operating theatre. I wondered how many other testicles had been removed that day and what was their record. *Are they removing testicles as fast as eggs at a chicken factory?*

I spent a couple of hours in a bed on the outpatient's ward to make sure everything had gone ok. I took a shameless hospital thumbs up selfie for Facebook and waited round long enough for my hospital lunch of jacket potato and cheese.

As I mentioned before, the surgeon doesn't cut open your ball bag and extract the testicle from your scrotum. They incise you horizontally just below your waist band and pull the testicle up and out like a clown and their never-ending handkerchief-from-pocket trick. Afterwards, it is sore!

Due to some nerve damage around the scar, you may feel some numbness in the crotch region, which can last for quite some time. Forever, in fact. You must obviously keep the new wound clean and free from infection, and once healed, you can rub Bio Oil into your scar to make it less noticeable. After the operation, you will stay in hospital for a few hours to be monitored. You may be given some lunch but then that's it. They send you straight home. Not even an overnight stay for a removed testicle so it isn't that much to worry about.

Up until the operation, the only changes are psychological. Afterwards, there is a physical difference to your body. With that, people's physical changes around you can start too. They can start treating you differently, like asking if you're 'really ok' whilst tilting their head in that concerned manner. For most people anyway.

What happens to your sack afterwards? Does it look uneven? No, the one remaining ball takes up centre spot in your scrotum and hangs in the middle. In my opinion, it actually looks better. There are some advantages of having just one ball: it's more comfortable to ride a bike, you can wear skinny jeans if you'd like, and it's now only half as cold when you enter the sea. Two balls are overrated anyway.

After I'd been discharged, Dad took me back to his house where he'd set up a bed in his upstairs living room, next to his big bay windows that overlook Weymouth. Dad has one of those upside-down houses where the bedrooms and bathrooms are downstairs, and the living room and kitchen is upstairs. If you look right on a clear day you can see the sea and if you look left, you can see the chalky White Horse on the hills of Osmington.

I spent three days laying there, only rolling over to urinate into a bottle that the hospital gave me. My wound was so fresh that I felt too delicate to walk or descend down any stairs.

After three days of not having a poo, I was finally ready to go to the toilet. The anaesthetic drugs make your bowel system a tad congested and it had been brewing for a few days since the surgery. When I eventually went to the toilet, it made me bleed. I looked down into the toilet and there was blood everywhere. This added to my anxieties. I thought I had internal bleeding from a surgical mistake, or some form of bowel cancer. I phoned the doctor and he told me not to worry and that it was perfectly normal for a post-surgery poo to make me bleed. Yeah, not a sweet recollection but I said this would be no holds barred and it's all part of the unfortunate journey. It's something doctors don't tell you during any consultation: 'Beware of the massive bloody poo.' And it's not in any leaflets either.

Later on, during the chemotherapy stage, you'll also end up having some legendary farts. Even if you don't laugh at farts, you'll find yourself chuckling at these ones, or at least raising your eyebrows in amazement.

After three days of lying down, I was getting cabin fever and slowly going mad in Dad's house and in Dad's company. I hadn't been out the house for seventy-two hours and everyone was fussing over me. The fuss was great and needed, but it was also getting too much, and everyone was acting unusual around me. Friends came over, delivering flowers, cancer fighting almonds and Bio-Oil to rub into my new scar wound.

I hobbled downstairs to the bathroom and decided to check the status of my scar for the first time. The dressing looked like someone had stuck a large sanitary towel from my pelvis to the top of my crotch. I stood in front of the large bathroom mirror and pulled the dressing back slowly from the top two corners. It painfully ripped out any remaining pubic hair I had left. The first thing I saw was the biggest bruise of all different yellow, green and purple shades. My whole pubic region was bruised like a peach that had been kicked down a road and back up again.

Then I saw the edge of the scar and pulled the sanitary towel dressing all the way off. I stared at my new naked body in the mirror. On closer inspection, it looked like Captain James Hook had opened me up. I was expecting a cute little splice of a battle wound but it was more like Hook had impaled the pointy end of his weapon into my skin and gouged me open. I don't think even Peter Pan would have recovered from this. I examined it for over a minute, going through emotions and coming to the realisation that I'd wear this scar for the rest of my life. Then I thought, *At least the cancer is out now, nothing I can do about it, it could have been a heck of a lot worse.*

For a man, losing a testicle is upsetting. It's part of what makes men, men. If a man is nervous about something, then people use expressions like, 'Grow a pair of balls.' Or if a man is brave and confident people say things like, 'He's got a big pair of bollocks.' I couldn't fit any of those expressions anymore. However, I still think losing a testicle is not as bad as a woman losing a breast. Women's breasts are there for breast feeding and can be quite aesthetically pleasing to the eye. One testicle is fine. Testicles don't have a reputation as being aesthetically pleasing to the eye. What does it matter if there's one or two down there? So, grow a pair.

My phone was constantly alerting me to get well soon messages, but I needed some normality again. If anyone was going to make me feel normal, it was Rich. Rich is my mate from school, and a man of very simple pleasures. He's never left our hometown, never went to college or university, didn't move out from his mum's house until he was twenty-nine and passed his driving test at thirty.

Every Christmas, all the lads from school return to Weymouth from where they now live, like London, Australia, America, and Dubai. Some are company directors or footballers, and I worked at the Olympic Games, but Rich doesn't care about any of that. He just wants you to put another pound coin in the pub's pool machine and get a pint because it's your round, again. It's actually quite refreshing; no chat about life or work, just 'get on with it and take your next shot'.

Rich turned up to Dad's, dressed in his latest ASOS clothes delivery and his hair spiked forward. He'd brought a card. I thought that was considerate of him, but rather than a *Get Well Soon* card he'd got me a *Sorry For Your Loss* one and drawn a little testicle in the middle of the card. Classic Rich. After a chuckle at the inappropriate card, he showed me what else he'd brought: two plums and a bag of Nobbys' nuts.

'Thought I'd get you a pair of plums for the memories, and I heard you needed some nuts.' Rich handed me the items while trying to hide the smirk on his face.

I gently limped down Dad's stairs using the bannister for support, whilst trying not to bend my leg or waist for fear of opening my wound and a small intestine ending up on the carpet. Rich unlocked his one litre Volkswagen Polo with minimal leg room and drove us to his flat on the fourth floor of an apartment block to watch the Saturday football. Thankfully, Rich let me spread out on the three-seater sofa so I could lie down flat, and he sat on the other sofa because in his words, 'I don't want to catch it.'

We had two hours of normality watching football on his illegal satellite channels and not talking about cancer or surgery once. When the football finished, Rich got up to take me back to Dad's for dinner. Rich is set in his ways with his routines and one of the things he insists on is that he must always take the elevator from the ground floor to the fourth floor, but he has to walk down the stairs when he leaves and not use the elevator. Walking down the stairs is his only form of daily cardio exercise, he says.

'My scar's a bit tender to be honest, so let's take the elevator down.' I hobbled over to press the button for the fourth floor.

'Oh my god, you're so lazy, just take the stairs.' Rich walked on past me.

I was struggling to even move my leg, so I waited for the elevator, and Rich started walking down the staircase. I got in the elevator and a few seconds later the doors opened. I walked out, but noticed I was now on the third floor. *That's weird.* I got back in the elevator and pressed the ground floor again. A few seconds later the doors opened, and I was on the second floor. I got back in once more and did the same again. The doors opened, and I was on the first floor. I eventually reached the ground floor as it dawned on me that Rich had found it hilarious to press the button for the elevator as he walked past it on each floor. I walked out of the apartment block.

What took you so long?' Rich, with a cigarette in his hand, blew out a puff of smoke. He'd played this prank on me once before, but at that time I wasn't three days out of surgery and didn't have cancer.

We started driving back to Dad's and Rich took a detour to the post office to collect an undelivered parcel. He pulled up outside and gave me the collection ticket. I looked at him and pointed to my crotch as a fair excuse for not wanting to get out of the car.

'Af, just go and get it. I can't go in, I'm parked on double yellow lines here.'

I shuffled into the post office so slowly that I was overtaken by an old man going in to collect his pension. Finally, I reached the front of the counter and collected

Rich's parcels. Two massive pillows! I exited the post office with a pillow under each arm and noticed Rich and the Volkswagen Polo had disappeared. I looked down the road and he was parked one-hundred metres away. I hobbled down the road, got into his car and he just shrugged.

'Double yellow lines, mate. I couldn't stay down there any longer, you were taking ages.' He pulled out another cigarette.

'Can I smoke this with you in the car?'

'Probably best not, to be honest.'

'Ahh for fuck's sake, is this what you're gonna be like?' He put the cigarette behind his ear, wound up the window and sped off like Lewis Hamilton trying to get home in record time.

We arrived at Dad's and Mum was there, waiting to take me back to her house. She had bought a new armchair with a foot stool for the living room, the dogs were now living in the back room and my bedroom had been completely tidied.

'How's Rich?' Mum asked.

'Ahh you know, Rich is Rich. I'm not sure he believes I have cancer though.'

'He's a good friend. Maybe a little dim, but very loyal. Anyway, you'll love the new living room. Let's get you back home so I can look after you.'

13.   I Haven't Got This

Life Lesson: Be aware of danger signs.
Cancer Lesson: Don't push your comfort zones.
Song Choice: *Your Love Keeps Lifting Me Higher* – Jackie Wilson

A common post operation question is, 'Do you get to keep the ball?' The answer… no! They dissect the testicle (ouch), put it under microscopes and do tests on it to see how malignant the tumour is so that they can make a prognosis for a chemotherapy schedule.

However, if you want to play any removed testicle tricks on anyone, you can do what my mate John did. I received a great replica testicle from him as a secret Santa gift. He'd put an avocado stone into a jar of apple cider vinegar and printed out a pretend surgical label with my name on it. The night I received the replica testicle, I drunkenly left it on a table in a bar in London. Imagine being the glass collector finding that! My apologies to the staff of Zoo Bar in Leicester Square.

After the operation, your testosterone levels are monitored. After tests on your blood and the dissection of the testicle, the hospital will contact you with your chemotherapy schedule. There are over two-hundred different types of chemotherapy and your age, general health and severity of cancer will determine the intensity of the drugs. Doctors and people you don't even know might say things like, 'You have the good cancer.' Or, 'If you had to choose one cancer, it would be testicular cancer.' *If I had to choose?* Cancer is cancer and whilst everything is new to you, that's what you need to be aware of. The thought of chemo is the scary part.

After two weeks of rest and recuperation post-surgery, I was walking freely again. My scar had started to heal, and life felt pretty normal to be honest. The scar still looked devastating but if you rub Bio Oil into it each morning and night, then it gradually fades enough to become unnoticeable, or you just become used to seeing it every day.

Maybe I was being ignorant and naïve, but soon enough my brain and the universe gave me a stern reminder about the dangers of my situation.

The fact I knew I was going to have chemotherapy very soon made me want to live life to the fullest before I succumbed to what sounded like a nasty experience.

I was back in Weymouth, living with Mum and getting lots of attention. The messages of support were in full flow and Mum couldn't believe how kind people were being. Not just to me but also to her. They sent cards, letters and flowers, and friends and neighbours made cakes and home-made lasagnes.

Nas thought the support could work as a solution to my medical bills. She ordered three-hundred baby-blue silicone wristbands off the internet with the words *You Got This* stamped on one side and *We Have a Laugh* on the other. *You Got This* was as a result of the comments received on my initial Facebook status. *We Have a Laugh* was always something I would say when something had not quite gone to plan.

Missing the train: 'Ahh, we have a laugh, don't we?' Being late for work: 'Ahh, we have a laugh.' Getting diagnosed with a tumour: 'Ahh, we have a…' Ok, maybe not.

We posted on Facebook to ask if anyone would like to wear a wristband to show support and donate money towards my medical bills as a return gesture. Although I was now in the NHS system accessing free healthcare, I still had the Brazilian medical bills, extortionate emergency flight home and the UK diagnosis consultations to pay, and I was unemployed for the foreseeable. On the first evening of the Facebook status, there were seventy two comments and most people wanted to donate money for multiple wristbands for their whole family to wear. By the end of the night, three hundred wristbands had been allocated and we hadn't even received them in the post ourselves yet.

While I was struggling to move for the first few days after the surgery, Nas sent off the wristbands with thank you notes. Every morning after that, I woke up and wrote addresses on envelopes and thank you letters to the donators before walking down to the post office with a new batch. It felt like a job, but a purposeful job with a good routine. It definitely took my mind off worrying about the future and thinking about the past because I was focussing so much on the present. The last person to have testicular cancer and start a motivation silicone wristband trend was Lance Armstrong and his Livestrong bands. *Maybe I should start looking at race bikes and enter the Tour de France.*

I started getting gifts in the post like I had a nineties fan club. Mugs, baseball caps, mouse mats all with *You Got This* emblazed across them. My school friend Dean Record set up www.yougotthisaf.com for me to post blogs and receive messages. Julian was right – so many old friends came out of the woodwork and showed me support beyond my imagination.

People I'd only met once at stag dos sent me messages about my infectious energy. I had young people from my youth work in Essex say that I had influenced their life. Other people told me that I'd helped them overcome depression. Yet more people told me that my *You Got This* post had got them back into the gym. Three people resigned from jobs they hated. One woman said her *You Got This* wristband gave her an extra push during childbirth. Even two of my ex-girlfriends got in touch and told me their families were thinking of me. One that historically disliked me even donated for a wristband.

Any previous social anxieties or wavering self-esteem finally disappeared. People liked me, they actually liked me, and they were telling me so.

The winter nights had started closing in, and Mum and I were sitting in her new refurbished living room. She was on her new clean brown leather sofa – no dogs allowed – and I was in my new 'cancer' armchair with my feet up on the foot stool. In any other circumstances I might have said I'd become a spoilt brat, but I think the personal armchair was fully required.

I got a WhatsApp notification from Ed Smith, a friend I'd met at university when I was a 'thirst aider' on his fresher's year pub crawl. I hadn't heard from Ed for years, but he'd sent me a video message. He was standing next to two-time Olympic gold medallist, Dame Kelly Holmes. Ed introduced them both.

'Af, I'm here with Dame Kelly Holmes and she's got a message for you.'

'Hi, Af. Firstly... you got this. Just keep fighting, everyone's supporting you, and good luck with everything.' Dame Kelly Holmes finished off with a fierce punch towards the camera like she was giving cancer a knockout blow.

I smiled and turned to Mum on the sofa.

'Holy shit, look at this'

'Aww, that's a nice message, is that your friend?'

'Yeah, I can't believe it.'

'And who's the guy?'

'That's my friend.'

'Oh, who's he with?'

'That's Dame Kelly Holmes'

'Who?'

'She won two gold medals at the Olympics'

'Aww. Well, that's nice, isn't it?'

I put the video on Facebook and Instagram to see if I could get a better reaction than Mum's.

The next day I woke up to another message, this time from radio presenter Dave Berry. He'd sent me a video from his taxi en route to host his morning show on Capital FM.

'Af, You got this, I know you can do it, good luck man.'

Looking cool as fuck as per usual, Mr Berry.

By the afternoon, my phone started pinging with notifications once more. It was another video from a friend! Anderson Silva – Brazilian superstar and Ultimate Fighting Champion – was sitting in his car.

'Hey Af, my friend, keep your focus and stay strong, bro. Don't lose your energy and God bless you.'

One of the toughest men on the entire planet was telling me to stay strong! I didn't bother showing Mum, but he is one of the greatest UFC fighters of all time. The guy is a superstar and a double hard superstar at that.

Mum and I were watching TV again the next night and another video popped up. It was my favourite darts player Wayne 'Hawaii 501' Mardle at an exhibition darts match.

'Af... shit happens, my man, but... you got this. Good things happen to good people and you'll be just fine, don't worry about it,' he said, mid-match, in his flowery darts shirt with twenty-two grams of tungsten in his hand.

Another restless night passed, and I woke up late morning with a video message from Soccer AM legend, Tubes. From his car, Tubes gave a fist pump to the camera and said, 'You got this, Af, come onnnn!' As well as his motivational video, he also followed me on Instagram and commented on my photos. Legend! And a golf-life legend at that.

Receiving the videos from celebrities and sport stars that I'd always enjoyed watching kept lifting my mood. *This must be kind of a big deal,* I thought. More and more people wanted to wear my *You Got This* wristbands. I was waiting for the next lot of information from my doctor and what my chemo schedule would look like, but right then I was more focussed on how many likes my celebrity videos were getting and excited to see if there would be any more. It was totally surreal.

I had lost count of how many days I'd been waiting for my chemo schedule update, but I had a fun-filled day planned with an old school friend, Ryan Hill. He'd arranged to pick me up and take me for lunch at the local Beefeater. Ryan and I were in all the same classes through school and played centre midfield together for the school football team.

Ryan is a big guy. Not fat or muscly, just a huge wardrobe of a man. When he moved to our secondary school and joined our class, we thought he was a year eleven student who had been held back for five years. He loved football and could kick the ball the entire length of the pitch at eleven-years old. He went on to play semi-professionally for a number of clubs, earning himself a reputation as the non-league free-kick specialist.

Ryan arrived at my house in his big BMW 4x4 and as I opened the passenger's door, there was a red football shirt on the seat.

'Where shall I put this, mate? I don't want to sit on it.' I leapt into the car to show off my new freedom of movement.

'It's yours, Af. It's for you that one.'

I opened it up and it was a Liverpool shirt.

'Aww thanks, mate. You know I support Southampton though.'

'Yeah course, but check the back.'

I turned the shirt over, and it had the number *20* with *Lallana* across the top.

'Lallana?'

'Yeah, it's Adam Lallana's shirt. He wore it against Chelsea on Saturday.'

'What the fuck? And whose are all these signatures?'

'That's the entire Liverpool team. They signed it for you.'

I stared at the shirt wide-mouthed in awe. Adam Lallana was the captain of Southampton before he'd left to join Liverpool two years earlier. I instantly forgave him and couldn't stop smiling from ear to ear. I held the shirt in my hands for the entire car journey whilst thinking of ways to thank him.

At the Beefeater, Ryan and I both ordered the surf and turf as he insisted he was paying. We were soon in fits of laughter about old school days and changing room antics. Even though we hadn't seen each other for years, nothing had changed, and it felt like we were sixteen-years-old again. We talked about old teammates and where they were now. We laughed at situations we had gotten ourselves into and the following detentions that prevailed.

We decided to thank Adam Lallana by sending a photo of me holding the shirt with some impressive Dorset scenic coastline in the background. So, we drove to Portland and parked at the Portland Bill Lighthouse. It's like the end of the world up there. When you stand at the furthest edge of the Portland rocks, you can see nothing but sea. As you look to the horizon you can understand why people used to think you would drop off the end of the earth by sailing over the edge. It's also always the windiest part of Dorset and the waves crash against the rocks as the wind whips off the English Channel.

At the very end of the cliff of Portland Bill, there is a gigantic rock balancing from the end of the coast onto another huge rock stack that sits in the sea. It's called Pulpit Rock as it looks like an open bible resting up against a pulpit. We walked to the foot of the balancing rock, which is about eighteen feet high and nearly vertical. Carved into the rock about six feet up is a sign that reads *Danger, climbers do so at their own risk*, along with two memorial plaques dedicated to two unfortunate climbers.

'Let's climb it!' I shouted with one hand in a hole in the rock and one foot off the ground, trying to coax Ryan into doing something stupid like we did during our school days.

'Ok, but me first.' Ryan pulled me away from the rock and with ten large spiderman movements, he had scaled to the top.

I followed up behind him a lot more slowly, and crawled onto the summit. We were standing fifteen feet above the rock-hard coastline and about eighty feet above the sea. The waves crashed below us. The top of Pulpit Rock is about six feet wide by three feet long so one step in the wrong direction would mean falling to an almost certain rocky death.

The wind blew hard against my face and the waves made a terrific noise. My coat started to flap like a kite in the wind and suddenly I felt dizzy and my legs turned to jelly. My sense of adventure had rapidly turned into a heightened sense of mortality. I crouched down onto my hands and knees to have as much contact with the top of Pulpit Rock as possible.

'You ok, Af? You look a bit green, mate.'

'I can't feel my legs.'

'Ok, let's climb back down.'

'Mate, I can't.'

'It's only ten steps away.'

'Ryan, I can't, can you phone the coastguard? They can send a helicopter.'

'Af, deep breaths, mate. I'll go down and I'll place your feet in the holes below you. If all else fails, just fall on top of me.'

'Ok, but give me a minute.'

Ryan scrambled down the rock and made it look easy, getting down in less than ten seconds with his wide stance and bucket-sized hands. I couldn't physically stand, so slid on my belly to the edge of Pulpit Rock with my feet dangling. Ryan climbed half-way up again and placed my right foot into the top crevice, then placed my left foot into the crevice below. My hands tried to sweat but my grip was dried out by the Portland stone.

Thirty excruciating seconds later, my right foot touched the ground and I leapt off the rock away from the sea. I think that's what you call a panic attack. I'd never had one before. To be honest, I don't think I even believed in them. My body had frozen, and I'd had no control over my limbs.

Ryan took my mind off the whole situation by cracking one of our childhood jokes and asked me to pose with Lallana's Liverpool shirt for a photo to put on Instagram.

'Please can you not tell anyone about that, Ryan? I feel embarrassed enough.'

'Tell anyone about what? What you talking about?' Ryan pretended he'd instantly erased it from his memory.

We drove back to Mum's house and I thanked Ryan for my new football shirt and the eventful day. I went to my bedroom to rest as the adrenaline of the day was starting to wear off. I sat up in bed with my pillows built up so that I was vertical, and an hour later, an email came through with my chemotherapy schedule. I was going to be seen by Dr Wheater, one of the top consultants in the UK, and my treatment would take place at Southampton Hospital, over fifty miles away. *Southampton.* That was over an hour and a half's drive away from home. To get to Southampton, I would drive past four other hospitals on the way. I was getting treatment at the Premier League of hospitals. *This must be really fucking serious if I have to travel up there for the next nine weeks.*

I read that the first week's schedule would be seven-hour sessions on days one and two, and an-hour top-up on day three of the cycle. My chest started to tighten like someone was standing on my sternum. My breaths became shorter and faster like I was breathing through a straw. I've had asthma from an early age, but I hadn't had to rely on an inhaler for years. The more I thought about the chemo, the worse my breathing got.

I phoned Mum and she told me that she was at the fields feeding the horses so couldn't help right away. I phoned Dad and he told me to try to not worry about it and to think of something else. My breathing got more difficult and neither Mum nor Dad were taking me seriously.

Panicked, I called the NHS 111 helpline. The lady on the end of the phone could hear me breathing like a wheezy toy and I couldn't finish a sentence, so she called for the paramedics to come to my house.

Ten minutes later, Mum arrived home just in time to let the paramedics in. They rushed upstairs with an oxygen tank and mask and put me on a nebuliser in my bed. The two paramedics and Mum watched on in my bedroom. I hadn't been on a nebuliser since I was nine-years-old, but it felt incredible to breathe smoothly again.

Dad had tried phoning me, but I hadn't answered. Then I heard his voice downstairs and he came to my room to check on me too. I couldn't look up at him because I was focussing on taking deep breaths in and out.

'Is he ok?' Dad asked the paramedic who was timing my breaths on his watch.

'Yes, Afsheen's going to be fine, but he'll need to start on his inhalers again.'

'He's nervous because he has testicular ca… can… cance… and has chemotherapy soon, but it's not too serious.'

'Well, he's had an asthma attack tonight, so needs to be careful.' They were both talking about me like I wasn't in the room.

'Well, I think it's just nerves, he's nervous. It's not asthma.'

At this point, Dad's disregard for my asthma and cancer caused a flashback of my entire life growing up with him. Every crappy thing he'd ever done flashed past my eyes like a vivid memory showreel. Him leaving my mum, never coming to watch me play football and buying me gifts rather than spending time with me. I looked down my nose at the nebuliser's breathing mask and saw my own tears drip onto it. I was so angry. I fucking hated my Dad for that comment, and the paramedic didn't appreciate it either.

'Afsheen HAS had an asthma attack, and it is NOT just nerves. We will continue to monitor him,' the paramedic snapped back with pure conviction. I had never seen anyone do that to Dad before.

My shoulders went from being tensed up near my ears to relaxing back down, my chest sank to its regular level and my breathing eased. Dad fell silent and actually looked embarrassed, turning a shade of red. A medical professional had put Dad the great denier in his place. I love my dad but fuck me, he can be an arse. Thank you, Mr Paramedic.

As the show ended and everyone left me alone in my bedroom, I felt a true sadness weighing me down. I didn't know panic or anxiety felt this way: so physically demanding. Mum was all over the place and Dad wouldn't admit there was a problem. I laid there just looking up at the ceiling. I knew I had to start taking this shit more seriously, and I think Mum and Dad had just had a wake-up call too.

My phone pinged but I was done with talking to people for the day. I glanced at the screen and it was an Instagram notification of someone commenting on my latest photo.

You got this, bro. Keep going! – Adam Lallana

14.   Sperm Banker – Don't Touch It

Life Lesson: There are three types of fertility treatment.
Cancer Lesson: Chemotherapy can kill your sperm.
Song Choice: *Show Them to Me* – Rod Harrington

Testicular cancer is most common between the ages of fifteen and forty-five years old. That falls across some of the most probable baby making years of mens lives. Although you're a testicle lighter after the operation, you can still produce semen. However, chemotherapy can kill sperm and cause future fertility problems, so the NHS give you the opportunity to bank your sperm. This is done at a fertility clinic before any form of chemotherapy begins. There's still a chance you'll produce active semen after chemotherapy, but they highly recommend that you don't attempt to make any babies for at least one year after your last chemotherapy session.

There are three different ways to get your partner pregnant from a sperm donation: Intrauterine Insemination (IUI), In Vitro Fertilisation (IVF) and Intracytoplasmic Sperm Injection (ICSI). I won't go into the science but IUI is directly inserting sperm into the woman's womb. IVF is when they fertilise a woman's egg with a sample of sperm in a lab and once an embryo is produced they place it in the uterus. ICSI is when they inject one single sperm directly into an egg. You can attempt any of these as many times depending on how many test tubes you have stored in the fertility clinic freezer. It really is a miracle of science.

I was booked in for a morning of sperm banking at the nearest available fertility clinic. A nurse phoned me the day before to see if I was prepared and to talk through the process. Not THE process but to tell me I shouldn't be feeling anxious. If a sperm deposit doesn't happen on the first visit, then it's perfectly normal. She said it was very common for men to sit in the room for an hour only for nothing to happen and have to come back another day.

'Don't masturbate until you get here because we need as much sperm as possible,' she instructed me over the phone without any embarrassment in her voice. *Damn it!* I'd made the mistake of not saving my sperm because my thought process was that I'd produce new semen by the next day, and that would contain my fastest, tallest and strongest Olympic levels of sperm. Rather than a week's build-up where any old tadpole could hang around, I wanted my semen to have the potential to create the next Usain Bolt, David Beckham or Muhammad Ali. So, if you're intending to bank sperm in the near future, don't touch it until you get there.

After Dad's telling off by the paramedic over my asthma attack, he was upping his game and doing all he could to support me. This started with him insisting on driving me to the fertility clinic. Dad usually talks to me about his work, or Iran, or the fact I'm still not married, but during this car trip he mumbled random conversations for the hour and a half journey.

He talked about work and then finished with, 'So how do you think they do it?' I ignored the question and then he talked about a time when he thought he had cancer,

119

but it wasn't and finished the story by asking, 'Do you think the nurse will do it for you?' He talked about what he wanted to do when he retires (tending his chrysanthemums at the bottom of his garden), and then finished with, 'Do you think they'll give you a magazine to look at?'

I wished I'd had headphones to put in.

Thanks for the lift Dad, but can we not talk about me masturbating?

We were about ten minutes away from the fertility clinic and my long-time friend Sophie texted me. The thing about Sophie is that she's undeniably good looking. She's a real-life head turner. We met when we were fourteen years old and I was a waiter at the hotel she and her family were holidaying at. Every summer, her entire family would visit Weymouth from Birmingham in the school holidays and everyone used to look at her as she walked past. As teenagers, we'd talk all year round on the phone and then spend the best week together every July, until we were twenty-one and her family stopped visiting.

Since leaving our respective universities, we've met up several times and spoken pretty much every day. We had a brilliant friendship but I was deep within the friendzone to the point of no return. We had this agreement as teenagers that if we were both still single at twenty-eight then we'd get married. At twenty-eight and still single, we delayed this agreement until we turned thirty.

Sophie had texted to ask how the sperm banking had gone. I replied and told her I hadn't been yet and was getting nervous, that it could take up to an hour and it was very common not to produce any sperm on the first visit because it's such an anxious experience.

She texted me back.

Sophie sends an image: Boobs!

Wow whose are they? I asked.

Mine, you bastard, she replied.

I knew exactly whose they were because of the freckle by her neck and the necklace she always wore. I just wanted the confirmation. I'd been waiting fifteen years to see them, and they were more glorious than I'd ever imagined. Cancer was amazing!

'Hope they help,' Sophie texted.

I put the phone into my pocket and arrived at the fertility clinic with a semi-erection. I walked into the hospital bent forwards, trying not to let anyone see my excited semi poking out. I met the nurse and she explained what would happen before and after the banking. She smiled intently whilst telling me. I couldn't tell if she was trying to make me feel awkward or make me feel comfortable.

'We can lock your sperm in a freezer for up to fifty years. Anything after that, you'll have to pay.' She then listed the terms and conditions for my sperm.

'Crikey, I'll be seventy-nine by then.' I started to think I wasn't sure if I'd want to father a child at seventy-nine years old.

'Yes. Now, we can also put one person's name on your sperm depository in case you were to die. Whoever that person is can use your sperm after your death.' She continued with her list of provisos.

Going to the fertility clinic is probably a surreal and daunting time for most couples trying for a baby. It's equally as strange when you're there as a single man and your dad's in the waiting room.

'I don't have anyone to put down at the moment,' I answered.

'Well, if you meet someone soon, just give us a call and we can add anyone's name. We can also take them off the list if anything goes wrong.'

Christ, she's really doubting my relationship possibilities.

'Oh, but you can't put anyone down, it has to be realistic. You can't just add Rhianna or Beyonce.' She looked at me straight faced, without any sense of awkwardness.

My ego took over... *Does she think Rhianna is not realistic because she's out of my league? I could date Rhianna if I wanted to. Or does she know the stresses that Rhianna's pop career and world tours would put on our relationship, making co-parenting my new born child with Rhianna unbearable and too much of a strain for both of us? Yes, she must mean that. Or... does she just not want to do more admin?*

It felt like the nurse slightly enjoyed knowing it had come to this – me sitting alone in a darkened room and tossing off into a plastic pot. That's what she thought. I just couldn't stop thinking about Sophie's boobs. *Hurry up and finish talking so I can get in that room.* She explained that the banked sperm would be divided up into as many different test tubes as possible, to increase the chances of using them later in life. The more test tubes, the more chances!

She then walked me down the well-lit corridor, past my dad in the waiting room and to my selected room. It felt like a dirty walk of shame. I said my goodbyes to Dad on the way and he wished me good luck and shook my hand. Yeah, that's my life.

The nurse opened the door to a tiny darkened room and the first thing I noticed was the blue leather sofa covered in three-foot-wide kitchen roll style paper. The trolley beside it was on wheels and looked like it belonged in an old people's home. I noticed the medical bin had a foot pedal at the bottom to activate the lid opening. *There's no chance I'm opening the bin lid with my hands.* An oversized white clock ticked loudly on the wall next to a sink which had a mirror above it. I looked at the mirror wondering why it was needed. I expected many men had wiped the sweat from their brow before they returned to the waiting room, or stared themselves deeply in the eye, witnessing the shame and disappointment of the moment.

The nurse gave me a plastic pot the size of a shot glass in a packet similar to the paper bags I used to get my midget gems in from the local newsagents. She showed me in and pointed to an old green file on the trolley.

'If you need magazines, they're in the file, and the WI-FI code is on the wall. You have one hour.' She pointed at the clock like it was some sort of Crystal Maze escape room and if I didn't ejaculate in the allotted time then I'd be locked in the room forever.

I looked at the revolting sofa with the plastic pot in my hand. *Am I supposed to lay lengthways with my feet up on the side, or sit on the edge with my legs stretched along the floor? Do I get totally naked? Do I just pull my pants down?* So many questions to answer.

It didn't matter. Sophie's topless photo and the added excitement of a fifteen-year teenage fantasy coming true made the ordeal climactic in less than five minutes.

I looked at myself in the mirror to make sure I wasn't sweating and thought, *I can't walk out of here after just five minutes. How long is an acceptable time to masturbate in a darkened room with your dad waiting outside for you?* So, I opened up Football Manager on my phone and played it for thirty minutes. I took Southampton to FA Cup Glory and placed yet another trophy in the cabinet.

I left the pot on the window ledge where instructed and walked back to the nurse's office. She said to wait five to ten minutes while she confirmed if there was enough. She came back looking happy, clutching a piece of paper with my results on it.

'Well, Afsheen, the average amount of semen ejaculated can be between 2-5 millilitres.' She paused and looked at the paper as if she was about to announce whether or not I'd made it to judges' houses on *X-Factor*. 'I'm pleased to tell you… you produced 4.4 millilitres. Congratulations! With one testicle, may I add. Very well done.'

It was the strangest proudest moment I'd ever had, and 4.4 millilitres produced twenty-seven test tubes of the stuff.

Dad and I got back into the car to head back home to Weymouth.

'So, Af, how did they…'

'Just shut up and drive, Dad.'

15. Chemo – Round One, Ding Ding

Life Lesson: Be prepared.
Cancer Lesson: Fox's Glacier Fruits are essentials.
Song Choice: *Eye of the Tiger* – Survivor

You're off to great places, today is your day, your mountain is waiting so get on your way. Dr. Seuss certainly wasn't referring to your first day of chemo when he was talking about great places. The build-up to this day involves emotions, a nice new scar and banking sperm, but that's all nothing compared to chemo. This is where the real battle of your championship fight begins. The first round on your way to winning the title belt.

From the moment you walk through the hospital and follow the signs to *Chemo* there is a change in mood. Like a boxer on his ring walk, focussing and staring into the distance with tunnel vision, you might as well be wearing a dressing gown with the hood above your head. Like a fighter in the championship rounds, you might have to bite down on your gumshield, but remember… you got this.

You need to prepare for this day like you would a fight or any challenge. Prepare as many good things as you can and wear your most comfortable clothes. Maybe choose jogging bottoms instead of jeans as you'll be going to the toilet a lot! Take a good book or a magazine, films to watch or a friend to talk to. It's not a great time or place to be reflecting and overthinking. Pack your favourite drink and my number one tip is to take some Fox's Glacier Fruits. Other boiled sweets are available but you'll need something to suck to remove the unavoidable vile taste soon to be in your mouth.

I should also warn you about how you may initially react when you enter the chemo waiting room. Even though you will have had surgery and consultations, you won't have actually been amongst the cancer community so far. You'll walk through the chemo ward doors and be greeted by a waiting room of bald heads and cancer sufferers. Everyone looks gaunt, weak and incredibly sick and there's a realisation that this could be you soon. Women are wearing colourful bandanas and men are hunched over with their partners rubbing their backs. This is real now and you're part of it.

Today is your day, your mountain is waiting...

Dad and I drove the hour and a half journey from Weymouth to Southampton Hospital. Luckily the roads were clear for a regular Wednesday morning in the middle of October. We parked at the hospital car park and followed the corridor signs for *Chemo*. I entered the waiting room and shuffled slowly to the reception desk. I felt like a new convict walking into a prison to serve my sentence. I was half expecting another patient to shout 'fresh meat' as I walked on by with my visible health and full head of hair. In a few weeks' time, it would be my turn to look at the newbies walking in.

Chemo days start with a blood test with the phlebotomist and a consultation with the specialist to make sure you're 'healthy enough' to receive chemotherapy. My height and weight were taken as a baseline to check any weight gain that might happen if my body retained too much fluid. I took a numbered ticket from the ticket machine like I was at the meat counter at a Morrison's Supermarket and waited in my seat for a nurse to shout my number. 'NUMBER SEVENTY-SIX.'

That's me, fresh meat.

An hour after my bloods had been taken, Dad and I were called into my specialist Dr. Wheater's office to meet Gus, my new cancer nurse, and Julie, the ward nurse. Gus was slightly reserved and completely the opposite to Julie who was bouncing off the walls with friendly energy, acting like we were lifelong friends. She was so welcoming, so smiley, so motherly. Dr. Wheater explained to us that I was scheduled for seven hours of chemo that day, seven hours the next day and a one-hour top-up on day three. During the next week, I'd have a one-hour top-up at Poole Hospital and one more hour top-up in the third week of the cycle. I was due to have this three-week cycle three times over the next nine weeks.

After having my height and weight recorded, the blood tests, the consultation, and lots of waiting around, I was finally called into the treatment room by Julie because I was ready for 'THE CHAIR'. *Ahh, the dreaded chair!* There were twelve big blue leather chairs with wooden arm rests set around the room all facing inwards, and all but one contained a slumped patient hooked up to an intravenous drip.

Julie left me in the capable hands of a young blonde female nurse with blue eyes who'd just joined the chemotherapy ward. She had great banter and it was nice speaking to a medical professional that was actually close to my age for once. If that level of banter was happening in a bar, I'd almost go as far as saying she was flirting with me. But she wasn't. *Was she?* She was just a nurse caring for a cancer patient of a similar age and having a friendly joke.

The nurse asked for my name and date of birth (definitely flirting) and started to look for a vein in the top of my wrist to attach a cannula (still flirting). My arms were cold because I was only wearing a T-shirt, which meant none of my veins were showing enough for the cannula needle to penetrate. The nurse tapped away at my arm trying to encourage a vein to come to the surface before sandwiching my hand in between a pillow and a heat mat to try to make my wrist warmer. She squeezed a tourniquet around my bicep and asked me to clench my fist. There's something quite disturbing about having a tourniquet wrapped around your arm and someone tapping your veins like a crack addict. She soon found 'a nice juicy vein' in my wrist to insert the cannula needle into. It was the fourth cannula I'd had in the last few weeks and they hadn't become any less painful.

The cannula was attached to a tube that hooked up to the first bag of intravenous saline. The first forty-five minutes of saline were easy. It actually made me feel better, but then the toilet breaks started. Wheeling your own IV stand across the corridor makes you feel like you're a proper patient. Taking the stand to the toilets becomes a common occurrence and requires a thought-out plan.

I stood up, careful not to knock the cannula, fearful of it coming out or stepping on the tubing and ripping it out. I pushed the toilet door as wide as possible and backed myself up before the door could shut on me and the apparatus. I went to the toilet like this over eighteen times. I was up and down to the toilets more often than a cokehead on a drinking session in Weatherspoon's. I was averaging a piss every twenty minutes, thoroughly washing my hands each time because as your white blood cells decrease, the risk of picking up an infection increases. The chemotherapy literally kills every cell in your body, good and bad, so if you have no white blood cells to fight off infections, picking up something even from a toilet door handle could be disastrous.

I wasn't feeling too anxious for the first six hours in the chair. The nurse changed my clear IV bags every thirty to forty minutes and with one hour left of the session, she approached me dressed in full personal protection equipment with two bags covered in red warning signs. She wore an apron, face mask, goggles and gloves up to her arm pits.

'What's with all the protective gear this time? Bit much, isn't it?' I asked half joking but actually full of fear.

'Well, we can't let any of this stuff touch our skin because the chemicals are very dangerous.'

'So, it can't touch your skin but you're injecting it directly into my veins? Sounds fun!'

'Nope, this is strong stuff. It might make you feel a bit low on energy. It's going to give you a metallic taste in your mouth. We'll give you anti-sickness tablets but if you still feel sick, let us know and we'll increase the dosage.'

Within five minutes, the chemo started kicking in. It was the heavy shit. With every droplet I watched drip from the IV into my wrist, I felt the energy disappearing from my body. I could physically feel the chemo move up my arm and become warmer as it passed to the ends of every one of my limbs. The warm fluid made its way up to my head and finally produced a metallic taste in my mouth and gums. It tasted like I was sucking on the end of an old rusty metal pole. There was no shifting the tang.

Luckily, I remembered the packet of Fox's Glacier Fruits that Julian had recommended, and they diluted the disgusting taste with each suck. The nurse handed me a paper cup the size of a shot glass containing a strong form of anti-sickness tablets. I washed them back with a shot of Gaviscon as the most incredible heartburn started to form in my upper chest. I put my arm back inside the warm pillow so that I didn't have to watch the chemo dripping into my wrist and going into my system. I rested my chin on my free hand and slowly sank lower into the chair as my body became helpless.

I looked around the room at the other patients and they were doing crosswords, sleeping or talking to visitors. A song by Jamie Lawson came on the hospital radio called *I Wasn't Expecting That*. I listened to the words of what I thought was a love song until I heard one of the last lyrics: '…and when the nurses they came, said it's come back again, I wasn't expecting that.'

Totally disturbed by the words, I looked around the room to see if anyone else had noticed the morbid song choice of Southampton Hospital FM, but no one seemed to care. Maybe they had bigger things on their mind and weren't getting wrapped up in emotional lyrics.

The last few drops of chemo dripped into my arm and the alarm on my IV machine went off to signify my bag was empty. My energy had been sapped, causing what felt like a horrific hangover, but I still had the task of navigating my way home.

I lived over an hour and a half away from the hospital, so the NHS had paid for me and Dad to stay at the Jury's Inn hotel in Southampton for two nights. After a ten-minute car journey, I was lying in the hotel bed wanting to sleep, waiting for the hangover feeling to go away. Everything smelled disgusting because of the taste in my mouth. That hangover-taste after a load of beers, a dirty kebab filled with onion and garlic sauce and going to bed without brushing your teeth. Some might say a mouth as dry as Gandhi's flip flop. I stared at the ceiling. *New patterns, no new answers.* Deep in thought and self-talk, I felt acid come from my stomach and up through my sternum and then…

'Hiccup!'
Is it going to be like this for the whole nine weeks?
'Hiccup.'
I think I can handle this.
'Hiccup.'
My head feels furry.
'Hiccup.'
How fucking long does this last?
'Hiccup.'

I tried everything known to man to cure the hiccups that night. Holding my nose, downing water, holding my breath until nearly passing out. But I hiccupped for the next ELEVEN hours; that's like hiccupping all the way from Rio to London. I drank more Gaviscon than was advisable during the most restless night of my life. I was in a classic hotel chain twin room, the kind I'd stayed in on many nights out and stag weekends, but rather than the other single bed being occupied by a friend, it was occupied by my Dad. And he was snoring, like a foghorn!

Day two started with Dad swapping duties with Mum, who had driven up from Weymouth to take over for her shift. The sickness feeling wasn't overly worrying, and I just had a groggy hangover head. I've had some legendary hangovers in my time, and I wasn't on those levels just yet. I've missed flights in the past due to hangovers and sickness, so making it to Southampton Hospital from the Jury's Inn was fairly achievable with Mum and Dad's assistance.

I was booked into chemo chair number seven and hoping to see the same flirty nurse from day one, but Julie said she was now working on the ward upstairs for the 'overnighters', or the inpatients as they're medically known. I would be plugged in to the chair for another seven hours, with multiple bags of BEP chemotherapy (a combination of Bleomycin, Etoposide and the platinum drug Cisplatin) being dripped into my system.

Nas had come to visit with my six-month old niece, Aria. Mum and Nas rotated each hour to sit with me as Aria wasn't allowed onto the chemo ward. Sometimes a nurse would sit outside with Aria while Mum and Nas both came in.

With the blood tests, consultations and chemo, the visit to the hospital took around ten hours. Ten hours far too long. Friday nights used to be filled with shots of tequila followed by a Saturday morning hangover, but they were now filled with shots of Gaviscon and forcing down anti-sickness pills. The most physical pain I experienced during chemo was the cannula insertions into my hands and arms followed by the ripping of my hairs when the nurses took them out. I made up my mind that before the next hospital visit, I'd shave off all the hair on my hands and arms.

Day two of chemo sent my energy levels lower, increased the acid reflux, and made the sickness worse. I had another night scheduled in the Jury's Inn before I could go home the following day. After seven-hours in the chair I left the chemo ward like a zombie, dragging my feet along the floor behind me and finally flopping myself into a chair by the hospital exit as Mum went to hail down a taxi. My phone kept vibrating but I hadn't looked at it for hours through lack of energy.

I had been sent a video. I opened it up and slid into the chair almost horizontally as Anthony Joshua addressed me in his boxing gym, with his ripped muscles stretching his vest.

'Af, impossible is nothing, you got this. I wish you the best of luck with your therapy, stay strong and I can't wait to hear the POSITIVE outcome.'

Anthony Joshua, the heavyweight champion of the world was talking to ME! The Olympic super-heavyweight gold medallist said, 'You got this'… to ME. One of the toughest boxers on the planet was in my corner during my toughest fight.

I stood up from the chair like a boxer getting up from his stool in the final round to knock out his opponent. I stumbled towards the hospital exit and found Mum outside waiting with a taxi to take us to our hotel.

Five minutes into the taxi ride, a new sickness started to move around. Like an uncontrollable motion sickness.

'STOP THE CAR, pull over, pull over, please!' I shouted, hoping the driver would slam on the brakes.

He pulled over onto the side of the road and I stumbled out and vomited onto the pavement like a Saturday night piss head.

What should've been an eleven minute journey became half-an-hour and the taxi driver grew increasingly concerned, but he was a legend for being so understanding when he was clearly feeling helpless.

We arrived at the hotel and he carried our luggage to the elevator. Mum propped me up against her side and we stumbled through the doors into reception like a couple of late-night drunks. We reached the hotel room and I got into the bed fully dressed, laid in the foetal position.

Please let me sleep tonight, I begged.

16.   A Big Hiccup

Life Lesson: It can always be worse.
Cancer Lesson: Ginger is a natural anti-sickness remedy.
Song Choice: *Lose Yourself* – Eminem

'To die would be an awfully big adventure'. Peter Pan, the boy who never grew up, says this to Captain Hook as he faces almost certain death, only to escape his arch nemesis and live happily ever after.

No one tells you when you first get cancer that you're facing your nemesis and will possibly look death in the eyes. Previously, your thoughts around death may have extended to what songs you'd like played at your funeral one day, but that's probably as far as it goes. That might change soon. A cancer buddy phoned me when he was first diagnosed.

'I've got a 50% chance of survival,' he said.

'Stop right there. There's no chance you can put a number on it, so don't.'

We're all different. Cancer treatments are changing every day, more research is being conducted, and new drugs and cures are being found. What might have been a 50% survival rate a few years ago will be increasing all the time. Plus, it's down to each individual.

However, no one tells you at the start of your diagnosis that you're potentially going to experience the worst days of your entire life. But that's probably the case. We never know a true fear of death until it's at our doorstep and prolonged enough for us to think about what is happening. One time, I almost died when crossing a busy road in India. I was nearly hit by a bus, but it happened so quickly it was a flash-before-my-eyes experience and then I got over it.

Cancer is a long-drawn-out affair, which makes you think of all the things you'll miss if you were to die. But maybe that's your path in life. Fighting cancer makes you appreciate what you really want and love in your life.

Mum and I went to back to Southampton Hospital for my third day of chemotherapy before I could go home to Weymouth. By now I was feeling like I was in the legendary hangover territory. I couldn't sit up fully, I couldn't eat and I couldn't drink. There was another new team of nurses in the ward and I slumped across two chairs as I waited to see them. One nurse came to measure my weight and asked if I was ok. I answered with a half a grumble. She took my temperature with a thermometer in my ear and put her fingers on my wrist to check my pulse.

'I'm just going to check your heart rate is ok.' She timed my pulse against her watch, which was attached to her chest.

She walked off and came back with an ECG machine on a trolley and stuck ten ECG electrode stickers onto my body: two on my ankles, two on my wrists and six on my chest. Pressing start on the machine, she started taking a measurement of my heartbeat.

'Just wait there.' The nurse was off again for a second opinion. I wasn't going anywhere. She came back with Dr. Wheater, who had a stethoscope around his neck.

I'd never seen him wearing one of those the whole time I'd known him.

'Have you ever had any previous heart problems?' Dr. Wheater inspected the ECG graph results.

I had no energy to respond so just shook my head.

'Ok, we're going to get you in a bed upstairs and monitor you as you have an irregular heartbeat.' Dr. Wheater put his hand on my knee. I knew the hand on my knee was not a good sign. Every previous doctor who'd touched my knee was bracing me for something. I now knew this tell-tale sign, so rather than it settling my nerves, it made me even more anxious. This wasn't going to be good for my poor irregular heartbeat.

The nurse came back with a wheelchair. Other patients were now looking on. They'd probably seen it all before. I was the only one in there who still had a full head of hair. I could sense someone looking at me thinking *first timer*. I was wheeled through the double doors and out of the chemo ward with everyone looking at me like the young foolish drunk who couldn't handle his drink and was being escorted out by security.

As soon as I reached the corridors of the main hospital, the world started spinning. The rest of the hospital moves so much faster than the chemo ward and my anti-sickness drugs were suddenly wearing off. Mum ran beside the wheelchair in a panic trying to hold my belongings while keeping the sick bucket placed on my lap. Everything around me was a blur.

Suddenly, it felt like something had exploded in my head and I had pins and needles across my entire face.

It was literally as if someone had just put my head face down into a pile of drawing pins. The fluid couldn't stay in my body any longer and I started to vomit. A pink projectile vomit turned into a painful bile-fuelled sickness which ripped my stomach muscles, and snot dripped from my nose. I tried to hold it all down in case my irregular heartbeat became even more irregular, aware that my sick bucket was reaching its maximum volume. I was trying not to spill any onto my trousers or the hospital floor but my head was getting warmer and warmer.

The young nurse put me and Mum into an elevator. The doors opened and we arrived on the second floor by mistake. I immediately thought of Rich pranking me in his apartment and hoped he wasn't doing the same here. The overnighters stay on the fourth floor and we soon arrived. We made it to the inpatient's cancer ward and my sick bucket was swapped for a shot glass of metoclopramide, a very strong anti-sickness drug. I was lifted onto a ward bed and laid there, as still as I possibly could, then I was attached to another ECG machine while my cannula was attached to a saline IV drip.

I started talking to someone in my head. *Please let me get through this, if you get me through this, I'll never drink again, I'll become vegetarian, I'll go to the gym, I'll look after my body, I'll be nicer to animals, I'll apologise to everyone I've ever hurt, I'll tell my family I love them more, I'll never leave Weymouth again, just please get me through this moment.*

I wanted to open my eyes and burst into tears, but I feared that it might raise my heart rate enough to put me into a cardiac arrest. I couldn't even look at the ceiling.

Instead, I kept my eyes shut tight and thought, *This… this is the worst day of my life.*

The metoclopramide soon took effect and my body started to relax. The pins and needles left my head and I fell asleep. I woke up hours later and looked down at my body. Each limb was still hooked to the ECG machine and there were bloody bandages on my arms from the nurse trying unsuccessfully to find a vein. I felt a new level of groggy that wasn't going to go away soon.

The young nurse who had *definitely* been flirting with me on day one entered the ward and came to my hospital bed.

'Ahh, he's finally awake.'

'Hmmm…' I moved my eyes in her direction without moving my head.

'You know, if you wanted to see me again, you could have just waited until next week. You didn't have to have a funny turn just so you could make it up to my ward and be looked after by me again.'

I raised as much of a smile as I could but I was fully aware it wasn't much of a response. 'You're going to be fine after some good rest. Dr. Wheater is going to come and check on you soon, ok? Just rest and I'll look after you.'

I wished I had the energy to talk back but I felt like a corpse. I had nothing left, no personality and no charm. I was only supposed to be getting an hour top up that day, but Dr. Wheater said I would have to stay for three more days on the inpatients' ward. I thought the outpatients' ward downstairs was depressing, what with the gaunt looking sufferers and bandanas everywhere, but the inpatients was another level.

I slept, drank tea and slept again on repeat. Other patients came and went, all lifeless like me apart from one man who walked up and down the middle of the ward with his robe open at the back. I think he was homeless, or he at least looked that way. He was insistent on getting the daily newspaper and wouldn't sit down until it arrived. I slept so much during the day that sometimes I would be awake during the night. There was a man in the bed opposite me who was about eighty-years old. All night, after the lights had gone out, he would shout, 'SISTER… SISTER… SISTER… SISTER.' It was upsetting that he was in so much pain but by 5am it was as equally annoying.

I woke up on day three of my stay and there was a new man in a bed opposite me. He'd just turned forty according to the birthday balloon tied to his bed, and he had the same cancer as me. His name was Fred. I found out that it wasn't Fred's first overnight stay and I could tell he was not one for structure. He'd found a lump and left it a long time before getting treated due to 'being too busy with work'. He was bald from the chemo and wore thin wiry specs that made him look like a character from the board game *Guess Who*. Fred acted like a prisoner who was due to meet with the parole board for his release date back into the real world.

I woke up at 11am and looked over at him. He'd swivelled his bedside table across his bed and was dunking biscuits in his cup of tea.

'Oh, good afternoon, glad you could join us,' he said in that sarcastic voice used by colleagues when you're five minutes late for work.

'Morning, did I miss the tea lady?'

'Afraid so, my man. I would have given you one of my biscuits if you were awake but maybe next time.'

'Shame, what biscuits you got?'

'Ginger, of course. Helps with the sickness.'

'Does it?'

'Yeah, didn't you know? I'm drinking ginger tea, got my ginger biscuits for dunking, and I've got some ginger ale for later. It's all about the ginger, my friend.'

'I bet I can guess who your favourite Spice Girl is.'

'Huh?'

'Ahh, nothing.'

'First time in here is it then?'

'Yeah, it was only supposed to be an hour top-up but I had an irregular heartbeat, so I've been here for three days now. Not sure if my body is up to it, to be honest.'

'Ahh you'll be fine, mate. The old irregular heartbeat; I went through exactly the same. Your body will get used to it and you'll become stronger. Just make sure you keep taking the anti-sickness pills and the ginger, of course'

'Thanks for the advice. I'm really nervous, quite scared to be honest.'

'You'll be fine. What's your name anyway?'

'Af, and yours?'

'Fred. Nice to meet you, Ash. You drink do you, champ?'

'I do, but don't think I'll be touching it for a while.'

He put his finger to his lips like a teacher silencing their pupils, and with his other hand he opened the door to his bedside cabinet and pointed to a black can.

'Guinness, mate. It's full of iron, it's good for you,' he whispered, covering one side of his mouth with his hand.

Fred's bedside table held his laptop and a Chris Evans autobiography. In between receiving chemo, resting and waking up, he was still running his business. Cancer wasn't a death note for him, it was an inconvenience. He was too busy for cancer, insistent that the world kept on spinning so you had to try and keep living as much of a normal life as you could. Fred was older than me, with a more aggressive tumour and receiving a more intense chemo, yet he was STILL running his business.

I had been very low thinking that the world suddenly owed me a favour, but it didn't. What should have been three days in Southampton Hospital and a two-night stay at the Jury's Inn, had turned into six days in hospital with three nights sleeping on the chemo inpatients' ward. I was only twenty-nine, but if Fred could do it, I could do it.

Things were going to be ok. As long as I could eat some food...

17.   Food For Thought

Life Lesson: The more birthday cake you eat, the longer you'll live.
Cancer Lesson: Follow a healthy balanced diet for best effects.
Song Choice: *Food Glorious Food* – Oliver Twist

My chemotherapy schedule worked on a three-week cycle. Week one was the brutal week, week two was when I started feeling a little better, and by week three I almost felt fine. Imagine a 3-day hangover when you're still hungover at your work on a Tuesday, but it's prolonged over three weeks. But everyone is different and there are many different schedules.

After your doses, you might not feel amazing, so I'd recommend keeping your evenings free of plans on these days. The more chemo and medication you take, the more risks of side effects you'll have. If you're not healthy enough to read medication information leaflets, then ask a friend or family member to read them for you. It's important to know what possible side effects to expect, in case you experience serious problems. You can also ask your oncologist about these too.

Some side effects are worse than others and some are as simple as food cravings. In week two of my cycle, I'd never craved pineapple so much in my life. Pineapple chunks, pineapple juice, ham and pineapple pizza. Everything had to have pineapple on it. There are obviously worse cravings to have, but I wanted to eat and drink what I wanted, which to my annoyance no one was letting me do. I wanted a Chinese takeaway and a can of Coke. Instead, Nas made me a lentil soup with legumes and then salmon and fennel for dinner. Why does healthy food taste so bad? (Fennel is awful by the way.)

My Dad's wife made me some Iranian dish with 'healing' herbs in it and Mum's friend made me a vegan lasagne. *I'm sure all of the chemo drugs in my body are working against the tumour so why do I need to eat new foods that I don't enjoy?* I thought.

However, research does strongly show that diets can affect different cancers so you should definitely assess yours. Women eating South East Asian diets have been found to have the lowest cases of breast cancer and men eating West African diets have been found to have the lowest numbers of testicular cancers. So, ladies, I hope you like noodles and Pad Thai, and men, start ordering the plantain and fufu. There's lots of information out there on this so get stuck into some books and YouTube videos.

People made comments to me like, 'Should you be eating that?' and 'Hasn't that got sugar in it and sugar feeds cancer cells?', which only made me want to eat it even more. One friend bought me a jar of Manuka honey with strict instructions to spread it using a wooden spoon because a metal spoon would offset the pH balance and spoil the good vitamins. Another friend bought me a bag of edible bee pollen and chia seeds to sprinkle on my morning cereal. Fuck me, it sounded like a lot of effort. I continued on a diet of ignorance with a side plate of naivety, following Fred's advice of, 'Eat what makes you happy.'

I'd returned to Mum's house in Weymouth after my terrible week in Southampton. Fred was right – the hangover was starting to wear off, but I knew I had another hour top-up in a few days' time at Poole Hospital. I decided to act a little bit more Fred and live some normal life before I felt shit again.

I also started getting my appetite back. Until that point, the flavour in my mouth made every food taste like cardboard. Unless it had pineapple on it. *Hmmm... delicious pineapple.* The thing with pineapple is it is very acidic, which results in heartburn level 5000.

Another danger post-chemo is the very high risk of infection. Chemo wipes out your entire immune system by killing all cells in your body, including the white blood cells that usually fight infections. The best way to avoid these risks is to stay indoors and isolate, but that isn't great for your mental health. To increase my white blood cells and immunity, I needed a daily white blood cell booster injection. I had the option of injecting this into my arm myself at home, but due to a fear of looking at needles, a nurse visited my house once a day for five days to administer the shot of Neupogen (Filgrastim). This injection really fucking hurt. Proper dead arm stuff like a horse had kicked me.

A couple of days into being home, Julian, my mate who was also receiving cancer treatment, texted me to see if I was ok. I told him briefly what had happened at hospital and he said he was going to drive to my house and we would go for a walk. I'd only spoken to Julian in real life on drunken nights out before, but he turned up to my front door with his little French bulldog named Archie. I'm not much of a dog person, but I brought Mum's sausage dog, Toby, to join us on the walk too.

Julian and I walked up the hills close to my home that overlook Weymouth. Very few people ever walk this beautiful picturesque route, which has a bench halfway up and at the top to sit down on and enjoy the views. We spoke about life and everything in between. I was quite depressed, but speaking to Julian raised my spirits.

I told him everything that had gone wrong at the hospital and he knew all of the nurses I was talking about. He knew Julie really well and loved her personality as much as I did. I told him about Fred, and my sister cooking fennel for dinner, and my desire for KFC. I told him that Nas said I had to watch what I ate, but that she wasn't in my shoes so how could she know? I told him that everyone was trying to tell me how to live, but no one could relate to what I was going through, except him.

'You know Nas said I had to eat legumes and almonds?' I complained.

'Yeah, they are a good fighting food,' said Julian.

'She said I can't have cans of Coke anymore.'

'Yeah, I don't drink fizzy drinks, I don't drink out of plastic bottles or cups, I don't put sugar in my body, and I don't use aerosols now, only roll-on deodorant.'

'You're taking this seriously, aren't you? Nas said I have to change because I'm a cancer sufferer now, but I'm not suffering. We're not sufferers are we mate?'

Julian stopped walking and paused and looked out to Weymouth.

'I'd listen to your sister,' he said.

'Really?'

'Yes, this gets difficult.'

We both went silent. The awareness sank in that I had to do more to face this problem. Julian had been receiving treatment for nearly two years and was having a lot more difficulties than I was, but he was still doing all he could to help me.

We reached the top of the hill, to a bench called *Margaret's Seat*, and took a selfie together with Archie in my hands and the view of Weymouth in the background. I usually walked up the hill with ease, but I was struggling to catch my breath.

Julian was so calming and positive as we walked back down to the car. He dropped me back to Mum's house and met my mum for the first time. I can only dream of having social skills like Julian: a bright smile, a polite demeanour and a sense of humour that is so natural. He and Frenchie Archie soon left and we arranged to meet up again in a few weeks' time as he had chemo the following week.

Not long after being home, a nurse arrived to give me my latest injection of the white blood cell booster Neupogen. Mum had made a homemade sweet and sour chicken dish, which had an exaggerated amount of pineapple chunks added to the sauce. Ian, my stepdad, was over for dinner. He'd been in my life for nearly twenty years, since I was twelve years-old, but still lived in his own house across the road (Mum and Ian were taking things slow). Ian met Mum when I was starting my adolescent teenage years, so he took a lot of the brunt of my hormonal attitude, but he was the only person calm enough to do so. He dealt with the full extent of a teenager shouting 'You're not my real dad.' Usually followed by a kick in the shins. A proper Dorset country bumpkin, born and bred, but I wouldn't change him for the world.

I was half way through eating my dinner, working my way around the chicken while inhaling the pineapple, when a sudden shooting pain began in my thighs. The pain moved up towards my hips and all of a sudden it was unbearable. I put the spoon of rice down on the plate, hobbled from the dining table to the centre of the living room and collapsed onto the floor. I was rolling around in pain like a pleading Cristiano Ronaldo in the penalty box.

'Call an ambulance!' I shouted to Mum and Ian whilst holding my thighs. They went into a state of panic, not knowing what to do. The pain extended from my knees to my hips. I was convinced I'd dislocated my leg bones from my hip socket, that's how bad it felt. It was like someone was ramming a blunt knife into my thighs.

Mum ran into the kitchen and opened up every box of tablets that I'd been prescribed. Metoclopramide, Omeprazole, painkillers. Ian pulled on a pair of spectacles and started reading the leaflets that came with each drug, inspecting them with his specs on the end of his nose like a librarian. Then they finally found it: *Side effects of the white blood cell booster Neupogen can include severe joint pain and discomfort.*

I was in pain for about five minutes and it returned a few more times as the night went on, but not as bad. The side effects were fucking mental. Mum and Ian went on to read the side effects of every drug that I had taken and was likely to take in the future. They wrote them all down in a notepad, as well as the days of the week that I'd likely take each medication. They became my additional medical team.

This was the side that nobody had seen. It wasn't the social media positivity side. It was shit. This wasn't feeling better. This was getting worse. Pass me the almonds, fennel and legumes.

18.   Money On My Mind

Life Lesson: Pay it forward.
Cancer Lesson: Banks will freeze fees for cancer patients.
Song Choice: *Crazy Maze* – Des'ree

Number one hundred and seventy eight of frustrating things to hear when you have cancer is: 'My friend's uncle had cancer and he still went to work during chemotherapy.'

People that said this kind of thing went straight onto the non-empathy list I was formulating. No two people ever have the same car crash and that also applies to cancer. There are over two-hundred different types of cancer, different levels of treatment, and just in case anyone forgets… we are all different.

A problematic part of cancer is dealing with finances and employment, but it isn't in a doctor's job description to give you advice about that. Money can be a taboo subject to talk about, almost as taboo as the word cancer. But we all need money so why can't we talk about it easily?

You may have a good employer with a big heart and a healthy bank balance meaning there's no change to your salary. That would be a blessing. But, like a lot of people, you may be self-employed but unable to work, unemployed like I was, or put onto statutory sick pay which is a low amount of money to live on. I've even heard of some unfortunate sufferers being made to take annual leave just to attend their chemotherapy sessions. With debts and mortgages to pay, cancer patients need all the financial support they can get.

It's important to try and not feel guilty about taking this support. You didn't ask for cancer and you've paid enough taxes and national insurance contributions, and probably made charity donations in your life, and now it's your turn to receive some charity yourself. But please, if you're a friend or family member of a cancer patient, don't say, 'My friend's uncle's second cousin's flat mate had cancer and continued to work like nothing had changed.'

Seeing Fred still working while on the ward gave me the encouragement to try and function a bit more at home. Friends and family had donated money towards covering my medical bills from Brazil and the initial private healthcare in England, so I stopped advertising the wristbands. I sent the remaining ones out for free to people who had written to me with a personal story of cancer or mental health issues.

After my original *You Got This* Facebook status, an old college classmate, Hannah, got in touch. Hannah's mum works for Citizens Advice and supports cancer patients with applications for financial support. Hannah was an amazing laugh in college, and she clearly took after her Mum, Helen, who was also terrific entertainment. They looked and acted more like sisters or best friends rather than mum and daughter.

Helen visited me during week three of my first cycle, armed with a file full of financial support options. The first thing was an application to get Employment and Support Allowance (ESA), which is a form of being on the dole. It was £74.35 a week and because of the cancer exemption, I wouldn't have to attend the Job Centre to claim it. I'd never expected to be on the dole but there I was applying to be on it for six months, extremely naive about how long it would take me to recover.

'Your last chemo session is the middle of December, right?' Helen made notes on her A4 note pad using a pink pen which had fluff coming out from the top.

'Yeah, middle of December I should find out my results hopefully.'

'Ok. I've submitted your application to receive employment and support allowance, until the end of April.'

'I don't think I'll receive it until then, can we do the end of March?'

'Well, let's keep it to April for now, and if you get a job before then we can cancel it.'

'It's less about me getting a job, but I've got a place for the London Marathon in April and I can't claim sickness benefits and run a marathon, can I?'

Helen paused and laughed at me. I looked at her with a serious face and she turned to Mum for reassurance that I was joking.

'I don't think you'll be running a marathon anytime soon, I'm afraid,' she said.

'April is seven months away. If I get the all-clear in December, I'll still have four months to train for the London Marathon.'

Still totally bemused, Helen asked me to sign the bottom of the employment and support allowance application form. She had seen the effects of cancer way more than I had, but at the time, I was 100% convinced I was going to run the London Marathon in April for the third time. I'd just received my London Marathon magazine through the post with the confirmation of my ballot place. *Maybe I could run it in a fancy dress costume – one of those big novelty ball sacks?*

Of all the charities, I'd selected to run and raise money for Macmillan. But rather than looking forward to the prospect of running in their green vest and raising donations for them, I was now filling out their application form for financial support. Funny old game.

A few days later, Macmillan granted me a generous £300 towards living costs and to pay for petrol to get to the hospitals. One of the mighty benefits of cancer treatment is the free parking. Some hospitals even have designated chemo spaces, right by the front door. Another benefit is a prescription exemption card which means you don't have to pay for anything from the pharmacy for the next five years.

A couple of days after I received my Macmillan grant, I phoned up my banks and credit card companies. HSBC said they would freeze all overdraft costs for a year and Lloyds Bank said I didn't need to pay a penny back on my credit card for at least six months. Result. Turns out not all bankers are terrible humans.

I had no money left and no income but enough help to survive, and I had just one medical bill left to clear. After selling the wristbands, freezing the interest on my accounts, and receiving the Macmillan grant and the statutory sick pay, I had a little clear out to find things I could sell on eBay. I sold a couple of golf clubs I hadn't used for a while and some old clothes, but the thing that hurt the most was selling my red backpack that I'd taken to Brazil with me. I'd bought that backpack specifically for my South American adventure and I had to sell it on eBay for £50. It wasn't about the money but the sentiment of saying goodbye to that bag was like saying goodbye to my freedom. I hope it found a good home and is somewhere across the world now.

One night I received a message from Sue Dale who ran the British Rope Skipping Association. I met Sue at the 2013 British Rope Skipping Championships (yes, there is such a thing). Years ago, before knowing anything about national skipping championships, I'd uploaded a video onto YouTube of me skipping in a gym. I was wearing a white vest and had my trousers pulled up to by armpits, looking like a fool, but my skipping skills were fast. After uploading the video and receiving a few thousand views, YouTube suggested *related videos that might interest you* and I saw videos of the British Rope Skipping Championships. After a quick google search and a filled-out entry form, I had entered myself into the 2013 championships.

I drove three hours to Studley, Warwickshire and ended up winning gold medals in the male thirty-second sprint (number of skips in thirty-seconds) and the thirty-second double-unders (two revolutions of the rope in one jump for thirty-seconds), and a silver medal in the freestyle, which involves skipping to music with some tricks.

After meeting Sue, her husband Chris, and their daughters Beci and Rachael, who actually hold Guinness

World Records for jump-rope, I kept in touch and wherever I travelled in the world I would add a video to Facebook of me jumping rope and tag Sue. I've posted videos of me skipping in front of famous landmarks like the Eiffel Tower and Times Square, and my latest video was in front of Christ the Redeemer in Rio de Janeiro.

Sue reached out to me on Facebook with a message:

Sue: *Hey hun, how much are your medical bills?*

Af: *Hiya, my English bills were about £1,350 but we have paid them off with the bands thank goodness. I had bills in Brazil of £900 and my flight home was £1,850. I'm hoping I might be able to get £500 out of the travel insurance for the flights and £500 for the medical bills in Brazil, but the travel insurance company have been terrible so far so having to get Macmillan charity involved. x*

Sue: *That's terrible. Chris would like to put £1,000 towards the bills from his business, and he says the bald look is a great look.*

Af: *I don't know what to say.*

Sue: *You don't need to say anything. If we can help in any way, we want to. You're a good bloke and if this takes the pressure off a little then that's great. Xxx*

Af: *I really don't know what to say. I'm coming up to see you in the new year to give you and Chris the biggest kiss ever.*

I was totally baffled. I'd only met Sue and Chris twice in person. To me, £1,000 is a lot of money. It had taken a massive weight off my mind and lots of stress from my family too. Stress can be one of the biggest activators of cancer cells.

I'll never ever forget the generosity from so many people on so many levels. I wasn't asking for anything but sharing my story made people want to help and apparently, it was inspiring them too. Another friend gave me £250 and a year later, I wanted to pay her back. She refused and asked me to pay it forward instead. I wasn't allowed to say what I did or how I did it, but she wanted me to pay it forward and help someone else. So, if you're worrying about receiving help from people in any way, whether that be emotional or financial, try your best to not feel guilty. But make sure that one day you pay it forward.

I also had a few donations from boxing clubs that I'd supported in the past: Will at Chelmsford Boxing Club, Adam at Eastbourne Boxing Club and Sindy from Chadwell St Mary Boxing Club. Each time I was speechless.

Once my head was above the surface, I asked people to donate to Macmillan or a charity instead. However, two friends were adamant that they'd split the money they'd raised between a charity and me. John and Mundy were going to go bald after shaving off all of their hair. Their lovely, lovely hair.

19. Hair Today

Life Lesson: New hair grows back like baby hair.
Cancer Lesson: It's not 'just hair'.
Song Choice: *This Is Me* – The Greatest Showman

'Don't worry, it's only hair, it'll grow back.' This is the sentence you will constantly hear as a newly bald cancer patient. Friends and family will try to reassure you and at first you really do think *it's just hair*. Probably more so as a man. But it's not, it's really not... *just hair*.

It's a statement, it's an identity stolen from you by a disease you didn't ask for. You're a prisoner inside your own body. People look at you differently, treat you differently. There's no more escaping it. I'd had dodgy haircuts in the past, but this was different. The words 'it'll grow back' are purely just an attempt to comfort, but they quickly wear thin. *If you're such a believer of 'it'll grow back', then how about you shave your hair off, Grandma?*

However, there are ways you could take control of the situation and maybe avoid the depression: shave your hair off and get some cool headwear – baseball caps, woolly hats, flat caps.

Dr. Wheater had told us that at the end of week three of chemo my hair would fall out. It was a strange feeling because I almost felt like, *at least people will believe me*. Having a full head of hair in the chemo ward can give you imposter syndrome. It finally felt like I was officially 'joining the club'.

I decided I wanted to take control of my hair loss before it happened so I asked my mates if anyone would shave my head. Rich was the only one willing, available and the owner of a £30 pair of hair clippers. He came over to Mum's house with his clippers and some work tools. He immediately went upstairs and fixed my bedroom window. I'd told him the latch had broken and the window wasn't shutting properly, which was making my room cold at night. We set up a mini hair salon in the living room, with sheets of newspaper placed across the floor to catch any falling hair. We decided that a number two grade all over would suffice for now and gently introduce me to the world as a skinhead.

First, Rich shaved the top of my head without touching the sides, making me look like a monk or Friar Tuck. He then continued to shave the rest of my hair, nearly hacking away at my ears in the process. He started making the usual hairdresser chitchat while he shaved the rest of my head.

'So, have you got any holidays booked this year then? You got any nice plans for the weekend?' Rich worked his way around the back of my neck.

'No plans coming up,' I replied with my chin tucked down into my chest. 'Why have you got clippers anyway?' I questioned. 'You've never had a shaved head and always go to the barbers.'

'Oh, I just use these clippers to trim my pubes.'

'That's nice. So I've got your pube shavings going on my head? Fantastic. When did you last trim your pubes with these clippers, Rich?'

'Last night.'

'What the… I don't actually want your pubes on my head!'

'Yeah, and I don't want your cancer hair going on my pubes. What if I end up getting ball cancer? You'd feel guilty then, wouldn't you?'

'You are unbelievable.'

'Thank you very much.'

I held up a small mirror to my face and wasn't actually too fazed by my new look. The last time I had a skinhead I was sixteen years old with a diamond earring and a slit in my eyebrow thinking I was in the So Solid Crew.

Rich said he was going to neaten up the hair at the bottom of my neckline. He removed the number two grade on the clippers, leaving just the razor. With one fell swoop he shaved a massive diagonal line across the middle of the back of my head. Before I knew what he was doing, he had curled up the line to form a tick.

'Seriously, what the fuck are you doing?' I leant forward, trying to avoid any more clipper action.

'I thought you'd look good with a Nike tick shaved in the back of your head.'

'Mate, seriously, what the…'

'What? It's all going to fall out anyway. You've got worse problems than a Nike tick. Maybe you can get a sponsorship deal.'

'How is that funny? That's not funny.'

Rather than looking at my head and feeling sad that I would soon look like a fully-fledged cancer victim, I now thought, *I've got to go out in public with a fucking Nike tick shaved in the back of my head.* Classic Rich.

Two days after receiving my Nike branding, I woke up late after not sleeping until the early hours. I had tossed and turned before finally falling asleep at 3am. As the noisy squawking seagulls of Weymouth woke me up, I lifted my head to see clumps of hair on my pillow. I pulled at my hair and big patches came out in my hands. It was impressive – it didn't hurt like it does when someone usually pulls your hair. It just came out cleanly, from the very last follicle in my head.

I got out of bed, walked to the bathroom and braced myself before looking in the mirror. *Fuck!* I was bald. I was actually like a bald man. I pulled more clumps out of my head and wondered if it might actually be the wrong thing to do. I gripped the sink with both hands and stared into the mirror. There were no other words. *Fuck, I've actually got full blown cancer. I look like a cancer victim.* Not even shaving your head can prepare you for this. When you shave your head or beard, you'll always have some stubble. But this was a clean smooth scalp with nothing on it.

After a few minutes of staring at my new bald head and inspecting the real shape of my skull, I came to terms with it. *It's only hair, isn't it?* I went downstairs to show Mum my new hairstyle and she tried to act un-surprised, but her acting skills weren't that convincing.

We'd planned to have lunch later that day with Grandma and Grandad. Before that, Mum and I drove to Dorchester as I was due a blood test to see if my blood counts were high enough to go back into week one of my second cycle of chemo, which was coming up in a few days. Before we met Grandma and Grandad, I decided that

I'd wear my new cap that my mate John had bought me and sent in the post. It's a lovely flat cap that can be worn by an East End Londoner, a West Country farmer, or a bald cancer victim.

We entered the café and as we were late, Grandma and Grandad were already sitting at a table near the back. Grandma was reading the menu deciding what Grandad would like for his lunch, and Grandad was humming out the side of his mouth using his knife to orchestrate an imaginary brass band made up of the rearranged glasses, mugs, and salt and pepper pots, with the pepper pots being the percussionists. We took a seat at the table and I hung my coat onto the back of the chair just as the waitress came over. I ordered the jacket potato with cheese, and inconspicuously as possible so as not to draw any attention to it, took off my flat cap.

'Oh, that's different,' said Grandma with the same level of 'not-shocked' acting skills that Mum had shown earlier.

'Yeah, I woke up with my hair on the pillow this morning,' I replied.

'Oh well, it's only hair, it'll grow back.'

Grandad stopped humming, looked away from his condiment brass band, put the knife that doubled up as a conducting stick back on the table, and turned towards me. He looked at me the same way he did when I first told them all that I'd found a tumour. And then he started crying, just broke down in tears. My grandad was crying in a café because I was bald. My eighty-six-year-old Grandad, the acorn of our great oak family tree, was sobbing, with tears running down his face.

I'd never seen my grandad cry. He only ever smiled and joked and hummed. My family aren't overly touchy-feely people, but I extended my arm across the table and put my hand onto his hands. His huge grandad hands felt cold and he put one thumb across my hands too.

My Grandad was my hero growing up. With Mum being a single parent, Grandma and Grandad looked after me a lot. Grandad grew up during the second world war, told me the most amazing stories, and was the patriarch of our big family, and he was now crying at my appearance. Grandma wiped a tear away from his face with a handkerchief and then dabbed the corner of her own eyes too.

A lump formed in my throat the size of a golf ball. My heart ached and I felt gutted. I wondered if I'd even manage to eat my incoming jacket potato. I was making people sad just by them looking at me. Before, everyone had hidden it well, but now I *looked* like I had cancer, the emotions weren't being disguised. I put the flat cap back onto my head and thankfully the waitress soon delivered our orders and took the attention away from me.

Grandad dipped the corner of a piece of bread into his tomato soup before going into one of his favourite comedy routines. 'Excuse me, there's a fly in my soup… what's it doing in there? It looks like backstroke, sir.' It was a joke that always made me laugh, and Grandma rolled her eyes as if to say, *Who brought him along?* Smile, smile, smile.

I arrived home later that day needing some normality and fun because it was week three of my cycle and I knew that the following week I'd be feeling like shit again. Rich offered to take me to the cinema in town and picked me up in his Volkswagen Polo. I wore my stylish flat cap for the journey and as we walked from the car to the cinema, I again nonchalantly removed my hat so as to not cause a scene or make an announcement.

Rich caught a glimpse of my shining new head and stopped walking.

'Ok, WOW!' Rich announced his shock at my bald head.

'What?' I asked, pretending to not know what he could have possibly noticed.

'You've… actually… got it… haven't you?'

'Got what?'

'Cancer.'

'Well, yeah. I've had it for over six weeks now.'

'Yeah, but look at you, you've ACTUALLY got it. You're a victim.'

'Ahh, it's only hair, it'll grow back.' I said as I readjusted my hat back onto my head.

And we both shrugged it off and headed in to order a large popcorn ready to ignore the problem and watch a movie in silence for the next two hours.

As we got to the doors of the cinema, Rich took the flat cap off my head.

'It's a good job we're not going to watch *The Addams Family*, they'll think you've come in fancy dress as Uncle Fester. Let's show them your bald head. You can play the cancer card now. We might get free popcorn.'

20.   Chemo – Round Two

Life Lesson: You never know who you're inspiring.
Cancer Lesson: Your team also needs support.
Song Choice: *Alfie* – Lily Allen

I'm not sure if round two of chemo can be classed as easier or worse. In some ways it's easier because you almost know what to expect, but in other ways it's harder… because you almost know what to expect. This shit was hard. Week one of a chemo cycle was really fucking difficult and maybe you get used to it, but that doesn't mean it isn't the shittest situation ever. You know what's going to happen, well, you think you know. The thing is, you can psychologically prepare yourself for a shit week, but that doesn't mean the people around you will. *Time flies when you're having fun, not when you're having week one of a chemo cycle.*

A week is a long time when you feel like death. Lots of sufferers may compare chemo to a horrific hangover feeling. But week one of my cycle wasn't the hangover. Week one was that worst state of drunk, where you know you're drunk, you're conscious that you're drunk and you could vomit at any minute. It's that moment between drunkenness and the hangover, when you're in a taxi praying you can get home to sleep before you puke in the back of the cab and get an £80 fine. It's that moment in bed when you shut your eyes and the room is completely spinning making you feel even more nauseous.

But, rather than being a drunkard in bed with my eyes closed hoping to fall into a deep sleep, this feeling didn't stop for a whole week. Seven whole days at least. One hundred and sixty-eight harrowing hours. Ten thousand and eighty miserable minutes. At least with a horrific hangover there's the possibility that you had an amazing time the night before.

As you progress through chemotherapy, you become familiar with the processes and what extra benefits you can get with your 'cancer card' privileges. Like free car parking at the hospital and free prescriptions from the pharmacy, as mentioned before, as well as entry into the Macmillan Cancer Support centres. These centres are based in some hospital buildings and are wonderful places, especially compared to the rest of the hospital. Let's be honest, hospital waiting rooms are depressing at the best of times, but even more so when you're about to start receiving chemo. The Macmillan centres are peaceful and welcoming areas with nice comfy armchairs and books to read.

The Macmillan volunteers greet you on arrival with an offer of tea and biscuits. It's a great place for patients to chill out before or after their treatment, and a place of tranquillity for friends and family to relax. You can just sit there and read a book, but they also offer informal chats, counselling, wig services, hypnotherapy, benefits and financial advice, fatigue management and more. On some days of the week, they even offer treatments like manicures, pedicures and massages. The lovely Macmillan volunteer that welcomed us said I was entitled to six treatments throughout my nine-week chemo plan, if I wanted them, of course. Or I could choose to donate my treatments to family and visitors. It really is a great place to sit in and enjoy before your chemo so make sure to ask if your hospital has any services like this.

Another positive about going to hospital for chemotherapy is that all of the other patients are facing the battle alongside you. As long as you're not the drunkest person at the party then it's ok, right? No one wants to be 'that guy'. If you're not the patient that is slumped the lowest in their chair or bed then seeing others in bad situations can be the reminder that it could always be worse. At some point you might even meet someone who knows they're soon going to die, which is just another unique experience to add to the all-round surrealness of cancer treatment.

Due to the problems I'd experienced in my first week of my first cycle with the irregular heartbeat, Dr. Wheater had booked me into the Southampton Hospital inpatients cancer ward for a four-night stay, ready to begin the second cycle.

Cycle two would also last three weeks, with week one being the heavy week of three straight days of chemo, followed by additional one hour doses in weeks two and three. There would be no sleeping at the Jury's Inn hotel this time, which suited me fine. Although the Jury's Inn gave me my own space without some old man shouting 'SISTER, SISTER' until 5am, I was happier about the fact that if anything went wrong, then I was in the right place.

Friends had sent me books to read and given me account log-in passwords for Netflix and Sky Sports, but

TV was the last thing on my mind. I was booked in for another three days of chemotherapy and a fourth day for monitoring. The first two days would both involve seven hours attached to the IV drip and then I'd have another one hour dosage on the third day.

Mum had driven us to Southampton Hospital to be my support during this round. It was now November 2nd and the nights were getting darker by late afternoon. There was the usual pre-chemo routine of blood tests, height and weight measurements and a consultation, but this time I would have a chest X-ray too, to make sure the chemo had not affected my lung tissue. Whilst I was in the X-ray waiting room, none other than Fred walked in with his wife. Fred wasn't so spritely this time and looked ten years older. He wasn't booked into the same room as me so we wouldn't be sharing his ginger nut biscuits this week.

Mum and Fred's wife got talking and soon had a stronger connection than Fred and me. They'd go for coffee breaks together and talk about how difficult it was for them to cope. They swapped phone numbers and kept in touch throughout. I'd met cancer friends who were helping me and now Mum was meeting cancer support friends too. She needed that. We both needed that.

The X-rays of my chest came back fine, and we waited another hour in the relaxing Macmillan Cancer Support centre before I was called upstairs to my new bed.

I arrived at the cancer ward and saw my name written on a white board in big letters – *MR PANJALIZADEH-MARSEH*. I was in room C bed four. Result! A bed next to the window. The best spot. That meant I had control of the window being open or shut and also, I had something else to stare at other than the five sick men who were sharing the room with me.

I had a packet of Fox's Glacier Fruits on the bedside table, ready to combat any disgusting tastes which formed in my mouth. However, by that time I couldn't even stand the taste of my favourite red ones so that week's sweet of choice was Starburst. Usually, I was all about the red and purple starbursts, but even those were making me feel sick and I could only appreciate the green and yellow flavours. Something I never thought I'd say, but that is what chemo could do to your taste buds.

I was all settled into room C bed four and ready for the next four gruelling days filled with needles and fluids. There were six beds in the all-male room.

In bed number one, by the front door, was a bald man in his fifties. He was a very dark shade of yellow due to jaundice. He had prostate cancer and had a urinary catheter going in through his penis. I know this because he asked the nurse if he'd ever be able to get an erection again. Those hospital bed curtains are very thin!

Next to him, in bed two, was a young black lad with an afro in his twenties. He wasn't in his bed but pacing up and down the room like a tiger in a cage at a zoo. He was a first timer for sure.

Opposite me, in bed three, was an older overweight white man with grey hair and a very messy beard. I knew he definitely didn't have testicular cancer because his gown was open and both balls were staring straight at me. Every time he rolled over to reach for his drink, his balls were fully on show. His testicles were hairy and wrinkly, just like his face. It put me right off my ginger nuts.

In bed number six, also by the front door, was another overweight man in his mid-thirties. He slept on his side facing the wall and didn't move. He had scars all up his back from the radiotherapy treatment that he'd been having. Radiotherapy and chemotherapy – that must have been really tough. His mum and son were by his bedside. His son, who was a teenager, was saying that his dad was going to die, while he continued to play on his iPad. It was sad. Very sad.

Then bed five, next to me, was empty, which meant I could keep my side curtain open and make my small little cubicle feel that much bigger.

An hour after being plugged into my first lot of chemo, my friend Lilly arrived. She had caught the train down from London to visit me. Lilly and I had climbed a mountain in Nepal together a few years earlier and had remained good friends. Mum went to relax in the Macmillan centre, so Lilly sat next to my bed and typed up a blog for me as I recited it. Lilly has obvious teeth like Billie Piper and hair to her shoulders which curls at the bottom. Whilst in Nepal we trekked for eleven days and there was no phone signal or internet at any point. That meant a lot of talking and soul searching. After we finished writing the blog and had posted it to my website, we reminisced about our Nepal trek.

We hadn't talked properly for a few years, but Lilly told me that she had decided to go back to studying.

'I took this summer off not knowing what to do,' she confessed.

'Well, there's no harm in that.' I looked at the IV drip to see how much fluid remained.

'I'm going back to university,' she announced.

'Nice, what to study?'

'I'm going to do my PhD. I'm going to become a doctor.'

'What! That's insane. You'll be great, Dr. Purser!'

'Yes, well, it's a long way off, but you've inspired me.'

'Me? Don't be silly, I'm an idiot, you're intelligence personified.'

'I'm confident with chemistry and physics, but your outlook is always something I aspire to have. You're so confident.'

The alarm on the machine sounded to signify that my IV drip bag was empty. I found Lilly's words a shock or maybe it was the alarm bells from the machine. Lilly was level headed, not erratic, and her moral compass was dead straight, but... she was looking up to me – a fool.

I'd noticed that as I'd lowered my barriers to the world, whether in real life or on social media, people had started confiding in me. Some moments of honesty were great to hear, like Lilly's. They were inspiring, feel-good stories that would lift my spirits. Some people, though, just wanted to download their problems onto me. I became very aware of this. I tried my hardest to let those people know – in the nicest possible way – that I had my own worries to deal with. Those 'energy vampires' or 'problem dumpers' didn't always take my replies in a good way. I lost what I thought were good friends, but it made me realise that some friendships had been one way for a long time.

However, the majority of people who shared their problems with me were very positive. Sometimes the news was overwhelming. A friend said to me that when he saw my original Facebook status about my cancer diagnosis his reaction was, *at least he doesn't have to go to work tomorrow.* He handed in his resignation for his job the following day and sought out some counselling. He was in a dark place, but he is now thriving. You never know who you're impacting.

Lilly soon left to get the train back to London. I knew that after the last bag of the seven-hour chemo session was in my system, I wouldn't be able to function for a few days. So, I decided to go and see Mum down at the Macmillan centre. I wanted to have a cup of tea without the smell of hospital disinfectant and having to stare at the hairy bollocks in front of me.

I walked into the centre and the old lady volunteer said that my sister had arrived and was in treatment room number one. The door was slightly ajar, and she was sat back with her feet up getting a pedicure.

'Enjoying that, are you? My free pedicure.' I nudged the door slightly to see Nas reading *Hello!* magazine.

'Oh, you're here. You weren't going to have a pedicure, were you?'

'Well, I can't now, can I? Where's Mum?'

'She's in room two, but don't disturb her, she's having a full body massage.'

'What the fuck! Why's everyone using my free treatment vouchers?'

'I'll buy you a massage at a spa if you want one.'

I walked over to treatment room two and rested my ear close to the door. I could hear whale music and there was a strong smell of incense coming from under the door.

I sat back down in a big red comfy armchair and drank a cup of tea while eating a plate of Rich Tea biscuits on my own. To be honest, I was in no fit state to have treatments. The smells alone were messing with my chemo brain and making my head dizzy. My body was aching, so there was no way a massage would help.

It was great that not only did I have a support network, but now my support had support too. Thank you, Macmillan. We all needed it. Every hospital appointment that I'd attend I'd come back to a waiting room to see Mum, Dad or Nas asleep in a chair. Life can be exhausting enough without the stress of cancer in your family. Nothing makes you aware of your vulnerabilities like cancer does, and that goes for everyone who knows you too. So, if you're a friend or family member of a cancer sufferer then you need to self-care too. Go book that massage! You deserve it.

21. Music Is The Answer

Life Lesson: Music is the answer.
Cancer Lesson: Tinnitus can be a long-lasting side effect.
Song Choice: *Dog Days Are Over* – Florence And The Machine

Earlier in this book, I mentioned that sometimes you need to slow down in life and reflect. Self-reflection can be a very positive skill. However, there is such a thing as too much time for thinking. Sometimes you just need to turn the music up louder and forget the world. Music can be a great tool for motivation and a funky beat to get you out of bed.

One thing to be aware of is cancer treatment potentially ruining any favourite songs you might have. Music that you associate with cancer will become a permanent reminder whenever you hear it for years to come. There are certain songs that take me back to low moments. The smell of hospital disinfectant and the taste of pineapple trigger memories too. I can't suck on a Fox's Glacier Fruit without it making me emotional. So be wary of killing the enjoyment of your favourite songs.

Although music can be a temporary plaster for the low moments, once the music stops there will still be problems to overcome.

I woke up at about 11am on day four of being in Southampton Hospital cancer ward, room C bed 4, with a window view. The previous three days had been a complete blur, in and out of any conscious feeling. After Lilly left on the first day and I'd had my last bag of chemo, I had been completely 'out of it'. My energy levels were at zero and I had been bedridden for three days, unable to get to the toilet and having to roll onto my side and piss into a plastic bottle shaped like a wine decanter. Sometimes the nurses wouldn't empty them for a while, so I often ended up with six bottles of piss on my bedside table, next to my food and drinks. Fabulous.

I received a daily injection into my stomach to prevent any blood clots. This injection was the most painful of them all and left the biggest bruise on my 'fl-abs'. Hairy bollocks was still in the bed opposite me but now there was someone in bed two next to me. His name was Gary.

Gary was sitting upright on his bed wearing baggy blue denim jeans, a tight white shirt and a gold chain around his neck. He had tattoos all down his arms and one across his neck. He had headphones in, listening to some RnB, and was texting frantically. When the nurse arrived with his chemo drugs the first question he asked was, 'How long will this take? I've got a date at lunchtime.' There I was barely able to open my eyes and he was setting up his next date, on a Monday afternoon!

He got hooked up to his chemo drip and took out his headphones. I could still hear the music coming out of them it was that loud.

''Ello, fella. You've been asleep for ages, they'll be plenty of time for that when you're dead,' he said.

'Yeah, haven't felt great to be honest,' I replied.

'It's all in the mind, geez. You must be a newbie, you'll get used to it.'

'This is my second round, week four in total.'

'Week four? That's child's play, mate. I've been on and off the stuff for three years.'

'Three years? That sounds awful.'

'It's stage four lung cancer now, only got a few months left to live. That's why I need to get out for my lunch date, I haven't got time to waste sitting in here,' he told me.

'Shit. Girlfriend, is it?' I asked.

'Nah, mate, this Polish nurse from the children's ward.'

'What!'

'Yeah, bruv. You got *Tinder*, the dating app?'

'I had it years ago, but not anymore.'

'Get it, fella. Put your search filter to one kilometre when you get into hospital. ALL of the single nurses are on it, I've matched loads. Nearly one on every ward.' He grinned.

'I guess nurses need loving too?'

'Maaaatteeee, it'll change your experience in here, even if you just want to have some friendly chats with them. Nurses have needs too, pal, and it's better than staring at these four walls.'

Gary was full of energy, and testosterone by the sounds of it. He did have a fair point, but I didn't even have the energy to muster up a handshake let alone swiping right and holding conversations with nurses. He was the first person I'd met who knew he was on earth with a limited time frame, and he had decided what he was going to do with the rest of his days. He was dating nurses all day, every day. He was playing *Tinder* with nurses like it was *Pokémon Go…* gotta catch 'em all. Fair play, Gary.

The chemotherapy I was on had side effects of tinnitus and a reduction in libido. The loss of a testicle can also reduce levels of testosterone so a testosterone supplement needs to be taken to get you back to normal levels. Gary sure wasn't lacking in that department. Perhaps he could have been used for medical science – he was on heat.

Gary left soon after his one hour top up, not even staying around for his lunch. I picked at my roast chicken, eating very few of the vegetables. I then managed to stomach the ice cream that came with my apple crumble desert. This bit of food and a cup of tea gave me 5% more energy than I'd had for the last three days. I decided it was a good time to attempt my first shower of my stay. I stank and my armpits were offending my own nose.

The nurse put a towel, some shower gel and clean pyjamas into the shower cubicle. The shower room was huge. An entire bed could have fit inside and doubled it up as an en-suite. Directly under the shower was a plastic chair with arm rests. Not knowing whether or not hairy bollocks had been the last man to sit his naked ass on the chair, I decided to move it to the side of the room and shower standing up.

I put a random play list on my phone and placed it on the ledge of the frosted window. I got in the shower and the water on my face woke me up and made me feel alive. I had both hands pressed up against the wall like a drunkard urinating down a side alley. I was letting the warm water hit the back of my neck and watching it fall to the floor below me. Within ten seconds, my 5% energy levels soon turned to 4%, then 3% and then 2%. I sat down on the floor with my back against the wall and legs stretched out in front of me. The water felt amazing, but I couldn't stand. I slowly dropped further down until I was laid in the foetal position, the water hitting the side of my body.

Usually, I'm not shy about asking for help, but I am when naked and curled up in a ball. The thing about the previous three days of chemo was that I was on so many anti-sickness pills, I wasn't aware of just how bad I felt. Now the drugs were wearing off, I could feel every ounce of pain and sickness. I was fully conscious of my feelings and it was the lowest I'd ever felt. As I laid on the ground, I looked across the room, along the blue floor tiling, and remembered something my sister once told me: 'Sometimes it can feel like you're drowning in a puddle, and all you have to do is stand up for yourself.'

The song that was playing on my iPhone had come to an end and the next one started. It was *Dog Days are Over* by Florence and the Machine. My fingers started to tap to the beat, then my hand, splashing a tiny puddle on the floor. I made it onto all fours. My lips moved with the tune and soon I made it to my feet. Each verse gave me more energy. There's a part half-way through the song where the music stops, and a clap begins. *Clap, double clap, clap, double clap.* I put my face under the shower head like the water was giving me life, like a plant at the start of springtime on a David Attenborough documentary. I was coming alive again. I listened to *Dog Days Are Over* on repeat another four times before getting dressed and going back to my bed.

I was ready for home.

During the next few days of being at home, I had more visitors. Laura, Dave and Stef had driven four hours down to Weymouth from East London. Mum always wanted me to stay at home and rest, but I'd done enough resting and needed some country air. I wanted to take the guys to the iconic landmark Durdle Door, which is thirty minutes from my house. Being from East London they get super excited about the countryside and beaches, whereas I might take the coast a bit more for granted. I wanted to dazzle them even more with a coastal walk, which would take about an hour.

Dave walks with an East London swagger, but being on the coast was visibly out of his comfort zone as the south westerly winds coming off the English Channel kept blowing his side parting up across his head. It was flapping in the air like a Bobby Charlton combover. Stef works in fashion and it was slightly enjoyable watching her navigate the muddy patches and cow shit in her platform shoes and flares. Laura, who was usually so ladylike and eloquent, had decided that she needed to dress like a boy for a day – in a full tracksuit – in order to navigate the Dorset hills.

I love taking people on adventures, especially friends. Something small to you can be huge for others. After walking up one of the bigger hills with a steep incline, we all became out of breath and started to walk in silence in single file. Laura and I waited at the top of the hill and were soon joined by Stef and Dave.

'Can we put some music on?' Stef muttered, in between trying to regain her breath.

'Yeah, we need music.' Dave panted, bent over with both hands on his knees.

'Just wait, listen… listen to that.' I put one finger to the sky.

'It's silent.' Dave stood back up straight.

'Yes. Brilliant, isn't it? No sound, nothing at all.' I stood there, looking out to the sea.

There was a few seconds of silence.

'Nahhh, I don't like it.' Dave interrupted.

'Yeah, I don't like it either. It's too quiet, I can hear my own thoughts.' Stef looked down at the floor.

Dave got out his phone and played an acoustic album for the remainder of the walk. It was fascinating to see people out of their comfort zone. Something as simple as walking up a hill made people reflect and not want to be with their own thoughts. Months later, I found out that Dave and Stef were both in jobs and relationships that they didn't like, and it hadn't been a pleasant time for reflection.

After our little expedition and getting some photos along the Jurassic coast, Laura dropped me home in her Fiat 500 before setting off back to London. Every window in Mum's house was wide open, and music was playing full blast. Mum never played music, so this wasn't normal behaviour. She was having a 'spring clean' so I snuck in the back door and crept up to my room to get into bed without disturbing her.

The TV was on full volume as Westlife sang *You Raise Me Up*. After four minutes, the song started again. And again, and again, and again. Mum listened to *You Raise Me Up* for over forty-five minutes. God knows what the neighbours were thinking, but I knew that she was trying to find strength. Whenever I hear that song now my eyes always fill with tears. It's the most emotional song I can ever listen to. It was heartbreaking, but it was giving Mum hope.

I listened to *Dog Days are Over* every single morning for the next four months. Some days multiple times and on repeat. I was hoping that soon those dog days would be over.

Sometimes silence isn't the answer, but music is. We all just need a funky beat and to forget the world.

22. Man's Best Friend

Life Lesson: Lavender has therapeutic benefits.
Cancer Lesson: Dogs work in therapy.
Song Choice: *Hound Dog* – Elvis Presley

Right, I wasn't aware of this fact so it might shock you. Ready? Dogs… can smell… cancer. I know, mind blown. I'll say it again because it's that amazing: there are dogs out there that are trained to smell for cancer.

I learnt this at a recent dog festival I visited called Dogstival. Dogstival is the coolest dog show in town and provides a fantastic family friendly festival for dogs and dog lovers, according to its posters. The spectators are drawn to the main arena to watch judges pick out winning dogs such as 'waggliest tail' and 'best child handler'. There's every dog you can imagine from Great Danes to Chihuahuas, and Labradoodles to Cockapoos. It really is a great day out for all ages.

Mum, Nas, my two nieces and I took Toby our family Dachshund to Dogstival for a day out. As I walked around the stalls with Toby, one in particular caught my eye. An old man with kind eyes was handing out flyers for a charity called Medical Detection Dogs. He told me that the charity were training dogs to smell for malaria, Covid-19 and a number of cancers. Some dogs could even sense when people were about to have an epileptic seizure.

He showed me the flyers that confirmed the dogs could smell types of cancer. I was speechless and happily handed over £5 for a dog-shaped car air freshener as a small donation to the charity. I then thought, *Ok, I've got some questions*. Firstly, why would anyone need a dog to smell cancer? And secondly, would it be a less stressful way of being told you have cancer, or would it be more upsetting?

Imagine attending your first Dogstival, having a lovely day out, then as you walk past the Medical Detection Dogs stand, one of the dogs just starts jumping up at you and barking at your heels.

'Aww, he's cute. What's his name?'

'Urmm, sir, this is Bruno and he sniffs out cancer. Have you been to the doctors recently? He seems to be sniffing a lot around your prostate.'

Would that be a less ruthless way of finding out you have cancer – a cute Labrador sniffing around your tumour?

'I'm sorry, Mr. Smith, you have stage four lung cancer, but look at Bruno waggling his little tail. Feel free to stroke him.'

Another question that came to mind was, *What doctor or medical specialist said, 'You know what, I'm not going to do blood tests or CT scans today. Nurse, fetch the dog, will you?'* Urmm, no. I think I'd like the blood test please.

Of course, after looking into this further, I found that medical detection dogs are used as a less invasive diagnostic. Not everyone accepts needles, radiation and CT Scans. Dogs have so many more positives other than just companionship. There are dogs for the blind, hearing dogs and dogs for anxiety. I was never huge a dog lover. I appreciated dogs but I'd never been one of those people who had to stop and stroke them and talk in a high-pitched baby-talking voice whenever they saw a dog. I used to find that weird to be honest. But boy, did that change.

Mum and I travelled to Poole Hospital, about forty-five minutes from home, to receive my one hour top up of chemo for my second week of my second cycle. We arrived early in the morning and my blood test came back successful that I'd be ok for *the chair*.

Poole Hospital is much quieter than Southampton and has a totally different vibe. In the bigger city hospitals, you can become a number on the conveyor belt of sickness, but in the small hospitals like Poole, it's more intimate with a personal touch. Everyone calls you by your first name.

We met with Dr. Geldhart and my cancer nurse, Stephanie. Dr. Geldhart asked how things were going so far and about my experiences at Southampton Hospital with Dr. Wheater. Stephanie was amazing! Like all nurses, she went that extra mile and gave us a direct line to call her on and an email address if it wasn't an emergency. To be honest, it was a game changer in terms of lowering any anxieties I'd had. I knew that if I had a rough night or painful side effects, I could email Stephanie just to make sure I wasn't dying.

On the cancer ward, in the only chemo room, I took up my position in chair number three, which was next to the window – perfect. As I was only scheduled for a one hour session, no entertainment was needed. By the time the cannula had gone into a vein, it wasn't long before it was coming out again. It was like the short haul flight version of chemo: after take-off you feel a little turbulence and then you're coming back down to land. It was certainly less brutal than the seven hour session, but I was still only flying Ryan Air, and sitting at the back of the plane next to the toilets.

After yet another painful cannula incision, I relaxed into my chair for the upcoming hour, watching the chemo drip from the bag into my arm. There were a few other patients in the room, but one in particular took my attention. A lady in her early fifties had her eyes shut, her feet up on a foot stool, and was receiving a foot massage from another lady sitting on a chair in front of her.

'Is it my turn next?' I joked to the lady in the chemo chair.

'Have you booked?' Without opening her eyes, she answered in a posh accent like she'd just come in from the manor house.

'I've got to book? Oh, I was just joking.'

'Yes, Janet is a lovely lady, but you must book.'

Volunteering on the chemo ward for the day, Janet rubbed deep into the soul of the other patient.

'I'm sorry, I don't have time today, but I'll be back again next week. Mrs. Knottage is my last patient and then I need to go home. If you're in next Tuesday I can give you a massage then.'

Janet sounded like the loveliest lady and looked at me whilst continuing to rub the hard cracked feet of Mrs. Knottage.

I couldn't believe what I was hearing, or seeing. A woman who actually came to the hospital to give patients foot massages. How lovely is that? I knew I would be back at Poole Hospital in another three weeks, so I booked into Janet's diary for a foot massage during my future chemo session.

Before leaving, Janet gave me a nasal stick to put up my nose if I ever had trouble sleeping. It was lavender and smelled like springtime.

'Two sniffs of that up each nostril before bed and you'll have a calmer night's sleep,' she said and put a sticky label onto the nasal stick with the word *Lavender*. 'It's been known to decrease anxiety levels in mice.'

Rather than thanking Janet properly, my mind wandered off.

How has someone tested the anxiety levels of mice? I drifted into a daydream about an anxious mouse lying on a tiny counselling couch telling a mouse counsellor all his mousey problems.

'I have anxiety that I'm going to walk towards delicious cheese, and it will be attached to a mouse trap,' the anxious mouse would say to the counsellor mouse.

'Here, smell this lavender.'

'Ahh, that's better, my anxiety has vanished.' And off the mouse would go to find more cheese.

Mum said my name loudly to snap me back to reality, and told me to thank Janet properly. I said that I was looking forward to my future foot massage and my calmer night's sleep.

Posh Mrs. Knottage told me that the next chemo ward volunteer was arriving soon, and even though I hadn't booked, I would be able to access her services.

Into the room walked an older lady in her seventies with a big black poodle. I'd never seen a dog like it before. She was majestic. This dog didn't walk, she pranced. Like a horse doing dressage. She was wearing a blue harness which had *Hi, my name is Poppy* written on it.

I've never had to stop what I was doing and pet a dog, but Poppy was different. She glided over to my chair and put her head next to my hand. I leaned forward and stroked her head. She had the dog equivalent of an afro! It was fluffy, like a cloud. Every time I stroked her head, her hair bounced back up. I could not take my eyes off the most fantastic looking dog I'd ever seen.

Poppy's owner had lost a member of her family to cancer and now visited the hospital once a week with Poppy to make patients happy. These volunteers were true selfless angels. The mood was lifted in the chemo ward and not just with the patients, but the staff too.

At the end of the hour of chemo, I started to feel groggy. My energy levels went down and the sour taste in my mouth returned. I went home to rest as it was the lowest night of the round two cycle. That week's food craving was cheese. Cheese on toast, cheese and biscuits, jacket potato with extra cheese, macaroni and cheese, chips and cheese, cheese sandwich, cheese and onion crisps. Everything had to be smothered in a delicious cheese flavour.

After a dinner of cheese fondue and four cheese pizza, I sat in the lounge in my cancer chair to watch my favourite TV programme *Gogglebox*. I started to feel depressed and anxiety was setting in. The night's sleep after a chemo session was never a good night's sleep. It wasn't the sleeping part that I dreaded but waking up the next day. It was the worst I'd feel because the anti-sickness drugs had worn off during the night. I was so fearful of that feeling that I wouldn't go to sleep until 4am or 5am. I'd never had anxiety before, but I knew this was it.

I got the lavender nasal stick that Janet had given me out of my pocket and sniffed it as much as I could. With each sniff I could feel my anxiety going down while thinking of anxious mouse and counsellor mouse. Then the lounge door opened, and I heard the pitter patter of Toby's footsteps. In he ran, waddling his little Dachshund bottom. He stood at the bottom of my cancer chair, and then with an almighty leap, jumped up and curled onto my lap. I stroked Toby whilst watching the TV and he soon made it a regular thing, every day and every night. He would sit on me for hours, cuddling up into me. My new best friend. Toby was the perfect size to snuggle onto my lap. He looked deep into my eyes like he knew I was sad, but that he was going to be there for me. My tone of voice changed into that baby-talking voice as I said, 'Hellooooo Toby.' We've never looked back and have remained best mates ever since.

I now have to stroke every dog I see and talk to them in THAT voice. We don't deserve dogs. The most loyal animal we could ever ask for. Fuck cats though; arrogant pricks.

Sleep and rest are the main ingredients for good cancer treatment recovery. Now I had my lavender smelling stick, nurse Stephanie on speed dial and Toby by my side, I no longer feared sleep. With the right sleep, I would feel comfortable enough to exercise my body. Or at least, that's what I thought.

23. Healthy Body

Life Lesson: The more you move, the more you lose.
Cancer Lesson: Do what you can, but listen to your body.
Song Choice: *Everybody Dance* – Chic

Exercise is the most under prescribed drug in the world. According to the World Health Organisation the definition of health is a complete state of physical, mental and social well being. You can't be a full picture of health unless you have ticked all three. It's important that you're as healthy as possible when it comes to fighting cancer to give yourself the best possible journey. This also applies to your support network and the people around you. Unfortunately, surgery, chemotherapy and psychological trauma will all have detrimental effects on your body's health, and the only person who can truly listen to your body is yourself.

Nile Rogers, the front man of the band Chic, said that after he beat cancer, he just walked for two years. He believed his only way back to physical and mental health was to walk. If you're reading this before beginning any chemotherapy treatment, I would suggest doing what you can now to increase your body's health and its ability to fight disease.

One of the worst side effects that my body suffered due to chemotherapy, was peripheral neuropathy. It's nerve damage that causes pain, numbness or weakness, mainly in the hands and feet. Unfortunately, it can last a long time after chemotherapy and becomes even more painful when the weather changes from autumn to winter. The numbness in my hands took away my ability to even unscrew bottle lids or flip open the cap of a shampoo bottle. Your cardio will decrease, your energy levels will become lower and your strength will near on disappear.

Men can also experience significant changes in testosterone levels, especially men with only one testicle. Low testosterone levels can lead to many physical and psychological changes. So, when you're feeling well enough in your chemo cycles, you should do what you can to exercise and maintain fitness. But at the same time, be aware of your new body.

Your support team also needs to remain physically and mentally fit throughout the ordeal, so they should start to incorporate exercise into their daily routines too. It will be problematic if your close contacts become sick and pose a threat to your well-being. You won't be able to spend time with people if they have colds or flu. For example, if someone gives you lifts to hospitals or cares for you then they won't be able to help while they're ill.

A social life will also increase your social well-being, which is just as important as your physical and mental well-being. Who knows, your resilience and persistence might even inspire people to face their own new challenges.

I'd received messages from friends running half-marathons and ten-kilometre races because I'd inspired them. I don't know about that, but they insisted I had. Many had raised funds for charities and tagged me in photos.

Nas probably hadn't run since school but even she'd been running weekly 5km Park Runs with friends, whilst wearing her *You Got This* wristband and a *You Got This* T-shirt. I was really happy to see her focussing on keeping fit, healthy and positive.

John ordered fifteen *You Got This* T-shirts for his Saturday football team to wear in their pre-match warm-ups before games. It was like a tribute to me and amazing to see the photos.

But I wasn't dead yet.

Neil Biles, who is my school friend Caroline's dad, ran his first marathon at fifty-six years old and wrote on Facebook: *I prayed for Af on the way round when things got tough. Af reminded me that I had the easy option, bless him and so true, enjoy. #yougotthis #wehavealaugh*

Nathan Walker, my old school friend and football teammate, was captain of Dorchester Town football club at the time. He'd come to my house in the week to collect some *You Got This* wristbands for the squad. He told me he'd score a goal for me in Dorchester's next Southern League fixture the following Saturday. I couldn't believe my eyes when I read the back of the local newspaper after the game – Nathan had scored his first ever career hat-trick. Three goals in one game. He was a central defender. In the write up in the Dorset Echo he'd dedicated the goals to me. Incredible.

I then had a phone call from Danny Dignum, a boxer I used to train with in Essex. One day in Rio just before the Olympics, I'd met Danny for some lunch as he was in the training camp with the Great Britain squad as a sparring partner. Danny had won multiple national titles as an amateur but called me this day to say that he was turning professional. His first professional fight was announced for 26th November 2016 at Wembley Arena. Not only that, but he'd had his boxing shorts customised with *You Got This Af* displayed in big gold letters on the waistband. He sent me a photo of the shorts, and I couldn't hold back the happy tears.

Danny had been boxing since the age of nine with his twin brother John. His first ever professional fight, at Wembley arena of all places, was live on Sky Sports and he had my name emblazoned across the front of his shorts. Danny knocked his opponent out in the second round and in his post-fight TV interviews he donned his red and gold T-shirt with *You Got This Af* beaming across the front. So did his coaches, team members and even Charlie Sims from *The Only Way is Essex*. It felt so surreal that everyone was showing me such selfless support.

I was so glad to see friends and family smashing their own personal goals. Nas running 5km was a huge achievement, especially with two young children. Neil running The Portland Marathon in his late fifties was massive. As was my friends raising money for charities.

I was inspired to do some fitness of my own, preferably faster than walking speed. I hadn't drunk any alcohol since my diagnosis so Rich and I chose to stay away from playing pool in the local pub. We thought about playing FIFA on his PlayStation but my fingers were becoming increasingly numb from the peripheral neuropathy. It felt like excruciating pins and needles pain in my hands, like I'd been bitten by some venomous spider. I had the dexterity of a horse's hoof so there was no chance my fingers could keep up with pressing the buttons on the controller.

We went to the local off licence so Rich could buy some beers for when he got home later that evening. I wasn't drinking alcohol during treatment, and I'd had enough beer in Brazil that I wasn't missing it, but I thought maybe a non-alcoholic beverage would scratch an itch.

'Do you have any non-alcoholic cider?' I asked, scanning the shelves of the store.

'We've got 0% beer, but I don't think we do cider.' The young lady behind the counter pointed to an untouched shelf in the bottom corner of the store.

'Ahh nah, that's ok, I was just wondering if you had any 0% cider really.'

'No, we don't. Just have a proper beer. You best have a good reason for not drinking, you big girl.' She looked at Rich for agreement.

Rich looked at me with an expression which said, *Don't say it.*

I thought, *Should I make her feel terrible here, take off my woolly hat and just point to my bald cancer head?* I wasn't feeling that cruel. But why did she have to call me 'a big girl' of all things? She was a girl.

'No, just on a health kick, that's all.'

Rich and I decided we'd just play badminton at the local leisure centre instead. He lent me his dad's badminton racket for the evening and we got back into his Volkswagen Polo, which stank of cigarettes.

Badminton was the first bit of cardio I'd done since being in Brazil. We started by playing rallies, just hitting the shuttlecock over the net and chatting throughout. My hands were starting to swell as the blood rushed to my palms. I didn't think I'd put on weight, but I was struggling to bend over to pick up the fallen shuttlecocks. I had to adapt and scoop them up using the racket, bending as little as possible. This sometimes worked but also resulted in me having to walk after the shuttlecock and attempt another pick up.

After fifteen minutes of hitting the shuttlecock back and forth, we agreed to have a match. The winner would be best of five games and each game was first to twenty-one points. I started the match and won with a smash following Rich's weak return. An easy one-nil lead. Matches between me and Rich were always close. Rich was the lazier of the two of us but he played a good variety of shots and had great power. I just ran around a lot and didn't give up.

For the next point, Rich hit the shuttlecock high and long to the back line of the court. I took three large steps backwards and hit the shuttlecock back over. Rich then caressed a delicate drop shot which just trickled over my side of the net. I moved half a step, but there was no chance I was making it with my sluggish energy levels. The same happened again for the next point – Rich executing a tantalising drop shot as I was out of position. He'd spotted that I was not as fast as I had been pre-chemotherapy and decided to exploit my weakness.

He exploited it for the next twenty-seven minutes. Rich thrashed me 21-7, 21-5, and 21-2. After every point he won, I waddled to the shuttlecock and tried to scoop it up with my racket or just knocked it across the floor to the other side of the court.

Afterwards, Rich took me back home to Mum's and came in to say hi.

'Who won tonight then?' Mum asked, handing Rich a cup of tea.

'Me, obviously. Af was rubbish.'

'Oh well, it's good exercise.'

'Yeah, it was good exercise for him picking up the shuttlecock all night. He really was rubbish,' he repeated.

'Didn't you go easy on him?'

'No chance. I wasn't losing to Uncle Fester. Can you imagine if I'd lost to him while he's got cancer? I'd have never lived it down.' Rich munched into a chocolate digestive without a degree of self-awareness.

It was classic Rich. He'd battered me at badminton, but it was good for my physical fitness and social well-being. It also made me aware that my body was not working at the same capacity anymore.

Rich has never played me at badminton since. Although he failed to show any empathy with words or going easy on me with a shuttlecock, he was there for me, always picking me up, shaving my hair, fixing my bedroom window, watching football with me and taking me to the cinema. He is a loveable idiot. Rich struggled to say how he felt, but his actions showed he cared. The messages I received from people were excellent, but nothing is more valuable than someone's time. And that's what Rich had always given me – his time. He'd never been one for changing, so to him I was still the same old Af and he was still Rich. I don't think we ever spoke about cancer once. As mental as that may seem, it was quite a nice respite from what had become the norm. He still dines out on the fact he once beat me 21-2 at badminton, but he doesn't mention that I was in my sixth week of chemotherapy at the time.

After badminton, I knew that walking was probably enough physical fitness for me. I needed to take care of myself and that also included taking care of my mind. Maybe even try out some holistic approaches, something new. If my body wasn't as strong as before, my mind still could be. I wanted something to believe in.

I mentioned this to Rich, and he called me the next day.

'I was thinking about what you said about believing in something.' Rich couldn't disguise his pre-joke giggle on the other end of the phone.

'Yeah, have you thought of something?' I anticipated his non-serious response.

'Well, I looked at your horoscope this morning and you'll never believe it. First thing it says… cancer.' Rich was laughing at his dark joke. 'Yeah, it says cancer, June 22nd to July 22nd, that's right by your fucking birthday.' Rich howled with laughter.

'Cheers, mate.' I laughed back at quite the clever joke.

'No worries. Chin up, baldy, see ya later.' He hung up the phone.

Maybe somebody else might have some more supportive mindset options…

24.   Healthy Mind

Life Lesson: You must exercise the mind.
Cancer Lesson: If you want different results, you have to try different approaches.
Song Choice: *Dreams* – Fleetwood Mac

If you can keep your head when all about you
Are losing theirs...

If by Rudyard Kipling is my favourite poem. I also love the fact that Mike Bassett recites it in the movie *Mike Basset England Manager* when the England football team are in turmoil. Nas had given me a framed copy of the poem when I first moved to university, which I had mounted on my wall. It's one of the best reminders that you should keep your head, be patient and *trust yourself when all men doubt you*.

Cancer and chemo can have a shit effect on your body, but you always have the power to control your mind. It's no use having a healthy body unless you have a healthy mind to compliment it. Life's tough enough without health problems, so you have to have ways of managing your mental health like you manage your physical health. Mental health campaigns are more prevalent in today's society but there can still be a stigma around seeking help and support. Especially for men.

We all have different ways of dealing with our mental health, so you have to find what works for you. You can't constantly escape your negative thoughts by playing music, running, keeping yourself busy or even worse, drinking alcohol. Eventually there'll be a moment when you can't avoid the thoughts anymore and they'll explode like an uncorked bottle of champagne, leaving a prosecco-stained mess everywhere. Nobody wants that. Sometimes the best way to deal with your mental health is to just sit and listen to your mind. I'd recommend finding a professional to coach you in how to do this, watching tutorial videos or downloading some apps. Headspace is a great app and talks you through various meditation and mindfulness sessions, as well as sleepcasts and focus exercises. (www.headspace.com)

Trekstock, the young adult's cancer charity, had given me a year's membership to Headspace, which usually cost £50. They'd also given me a three-month subscription to Now TV with the option of having movies or sports. I chose the Sky Sports channels, which gave me some entertainment when I wasn't feeling my best. Headspace can now be found on Netflix and there are also YouTube videos in breathing techniques.

Just like exercising your biceps, you need practice in how to exercise your mind. It doesn't just happen the first time you sit down and focus on your thoughts, it takes practice. You're potentially trying something that you've never tried before. If you were serious about training your body in a gym, you'd perhaps hire a personal trainer, watch instructional YouTube videos in how to do a bench press, join a workout class and use apps to structure a workout plan. So why don't people have that approach to mental health? When you run, you don't just lace up your trainers and run long distances; you gradually build up muscular and cardiovascular strength. The same applies to your mind and your ability to create headspace.

By week six of chemotherapy, while I was in the third week of my second cycle, I'd started to get my physical health back and felt normal again. I received another envelope in the post, containing a small box. I opened the small turquoise box and inside were four stones. I'd received some cool gifts in the post but a box of stones was a new one. I opened the accompanying handwritten letter from a girl I knew called Robyn Davis. We had spent our younger years and nights out on the town. I wouldn't say we were close friends exactly, she was just someone I knew, so this was an extra surprise.

In her four page letter she had explained everything about the stones. Except they weren't stones – they were crystals. There's something really personal about a handwritten letter; I don't think people send them enough. Robyn had written about how her life was going, that she'd always watched my life from afar on social media, and that she was expecting her first child soon.

She explained that the crystals were in fact healing crystals. I'd need to wash them in a natural free flowing river to 'cleanse' them and then put them on my window ledge to charge their energies from a full moon. She wrote that I shouldn't let anyone else touch my crystals because they'd lose their healing energies and I'd have to wash and cleanse them again. It sounded like hippy shit to me, but I was willing to try anything at this point.

So, I found a stream close by and 'cleansed' my crystals in the pure water. It was a pretty cool adventure for the day and something to focus my mind on. That night I left the crystals on my window ledge so they could charge their healing energies from the full moon. I was so touched by this handwritten letter from Robyn – someone I barely knew – and that she'd gone to such an effort to provide me with some positivity. It was so thoughtful that I would use the crystals as a thank you to her. I took them with me in the small turquoise box on every future hospital visit I went to. They still sit proudly on my window ledge to this day.

A few weeks previously, during my third week of chemo, one of my best friends, James, said that his dad wanted to pay for me to have meditation classes. James was a professional footballer. His dad and I used to travel the country together to watch James play away fixtures for AFC Bournemouth.

James's dad had recently suffered a major electrocution accident at his work and had become all spiritual about life. He quit his job as an electrician and went on yoga retreats and became vegan. He now greets us with 'Namaste' and meditates five times a day. He'd paid for me to have six one-hour lessons from a meditation and well-being specialist called Sharon George.

I was now on session four of my Introduction to Meditation classes. I'd go to Sharon's apartment and she'd welcome me into a zen-like room with crystals, burning incense and little Buddha statues everywhere. We'd spend the hour talking about what was on my mind and how I dealt with negative thoughts, and then I closed my eyes, focussing on breathing and meditating. I'd say I have an overactive mind and imagination. I'm not one of those people that can shut their eyes and fall straight to sleep. Even just shutting my eyes I'm like, *Ahh, my thoughts, my thoughts.*

Sharon told me to sit down, with my back straight and a good posture, and to close my eyes.

'Breathe innnnn… feel your body filling with air in your lungs… and breathe outtttt… if the mind starts to wander just bring the focus back to your breathing and… breathe innnnn… and breathe outtttttttt…'

I'm always willing to try new things but, at first, I thought it was absolutely mental. I sat there with my back straight and my hands gently resting on my thighs and secretly opened one eye. I looked around the room to see if there were any cameras or if James had walked in to announce it was all a stitch-up to make me look stupid. But it wasn't.

I had six one-hour meditation coaching sessions with Sharon and then developed further using the Headspace app. I was getting better at focussing my mind. Sharon taught me all different types of meditation and mindfulness techniques, and spoke about healing crystals and chakras. I was keen to learn all of the techniques to see which ones fitted me best. I tried all of them, but I had to draw the line at the stereotypical mediation technique of sitting on the floor crossed legged, my index finger and thumb touching to make a circle, while reciting, 'Ahummmmm… ahummmmm.' I wasn't far enough advanced to adopt that method but I could totally see why people used it. I wasn't going to be investing in any loose yoga pants with elephants printed all over them just yet.

One technique I did buy into was really focussing on my breathing; the movement of my chest and counting in my head from one to four and back to one again. Just thinking about the process of breathing and counting gives you a new focus and rests your mind. You could even change counting from one to four to thinking of words or a catchphrase, like: *you… got… this.*

I never thought I'd see the day where I'd be meditating and washing healing crystals, but it was a new level of focus. When I went to Poole Hospital for the last top up of chemotherapy of my second cycle, I sat in 'The Chair' and braced myself. This time I'd shaved my arms to try and take away the pain of the cannula plasters ripping my hairs out. The nurse cleaned the area with sterile cotton wool and that was when the fear and anxiety would always kick in – the moment the nurse rubbed my arm. I closed my eyes, sat up straight and focussed on my breathing, counting my breaths slowly, from one to four and back down to one again. I wiggled my toes and as I took deep breaths in, I repeated the words in my head: *you… got… this… you… got… this.*

'That was easy this week,' the nurse said as she threw the cannula packaging into a bin with yellow hazard signs.

I opened my eyes and the cannula was in my arm. I hadn't felt a thing. I had been so focussed on my breathing and maintaining a positive mindset that I felt no pain. Problem solved. I'd had so much time to myself the last few months that I'd been overthinking, becoming anxious and worrying, but dedicating ten minutes a day for meditation was the perfect mind exercise. Just focussing on breathing and nothing else. A healthy time to train the chimp.

I continued to focus my mind each time I had a needle stuck in me from then on. It got easier each time. My arms and hands were looking more like a dart board with the amount of scratches, needle pricks and bruises that I had on them, but at least I had one less thing to worry about.

If you can fill the unforgiving minute
With sixty seconds' worth of distance run,
Yours is the Earth and everything that's in it,
And – which is more – you'll be a Man, my son!
– Kipling

25. Chemo - Round Three (Missed Opportunities)

Life Lesson: Ask the question.
Cancer Lesson: Ask doctors to be clear with medical information..
Song Choice: *Belter* – Gerry Cinnamon

As the weeks of treatment move on, you'll learn more and more about cancer, drugs and medical terminology. This increased knowledge is great. In the early days of diagnosis, ignorance, naivety and denial might get you through the low points. But after a while, it becomes all about acceptance, action and taking control. You'll fight the cancer with experience, giving it the Ali shuffle, ready to knock it out once and for all. The entire situation can be difficult to accept, but once you take control, it becomes more manageable. You start to not look back as much. Of course, you can sometimes, to see how far you've come. It's also ok to look forward and set goals for the future, but you'll only get to those goals by achieving the things you can take care of in the present. One step at a time. The quickest way to get somewhere is often the slowest approach.

Cancer can feel like fighting in a boxing match. It takes the same preparation and dedication into beating your new tumorous opponent. If you were training for a boxing match, you'd train hard and increase your physical fitness. You'd get a boxing coach to be in your corner, as well as a team of screaming fans to cheer you on. You'd eat the correct foods and take in the right fluids. Boxers even use their positive mindset to get in the right frame of mind, visualising knocking their opponent out. All of these skills can be used to 'knock out' cancer too.

Beating cancer is much harder than fighting in a boxing match, or any other challenge come to think of it. A fight against cancer is not a fair fight. It punches you before the bell, gives you low blows and cheats with dirty tactics. So, don't pretend cancer doesn't need that level of planning. The minute you move into acceptance, all life's challenges become a lot more achievable.

It was the last week of November, Dad and I travelled to Southampton Hospital for chemotherapy round three – what we hoped would be my final cycle. Dad had shaved all of his hair off in solidarity and was sporting a new bald head. He was styling out his new look very well for a sixty-year-old Iranian businessman. We were both sitting in the front seats of his Mercedes completely bald. If it wasn't for my cancer bloated weakness, we could have passed as Iran's answer to the Mitchell brothers. Or the Persian equivalent of Right Said Fred.

In Iran, men don't shave off their hair, that's only what young children and the military do. It was a huge deal for Dad, but he wanted to show solidarity and be on the journey with me. I had a feeling that eventually my hair would grow back, but at sixty years old, it wasn't a certainty for Dad. He hadn't just shaved his hair short, he had wet shaved it with a razor. Completely bald. With his new look and wearing his blue *You Got This* wristband, he was completely living the journey with me. He would have plugged himself into the chemo machine if he knew it would have taken some of my pain away.

I had been sent photos from a number of friends who had also braved the shave and gone bald to support me. John, Pete, Dixon, Robbo and Mundy, all in different parts of the country, had taken clippers to their heads. Pete and Dixon had been receding and thinning on top for years, so it was a timely excuse for them to finally shave it and they've remained bald ever since. For John, Robbo and especially Mundy, it was momentous. They'd all had the thickest flowing hair. Mundy had even won 'Loveliest Hair Award' at university three years running! It was such a travesty to shave off his tremendous barnet that he raised over £1,000 for charity. I'm glad to report that his hair grew back just as beautifully as before.

It was great that the lads supported me by shaving their heads, but just as overwhelming was receiving a message from a woman named Christie who I met in India during the Rickshaw Rally. Christie had dark brown hair down to her lower back, but she'd cut all of it off and donated it to a children's cancer wig making charity. I just couldn't believe it.

Nas met us in the hospital reception and greeted me with a carrier bag full of food to munch on for the next few days. She knew I wouldn't eat any of it, but she brought it anyway. I had my morning blood tests done, and wandered aimlessly around WH Smith and Marks and Spencer trying to fill the dead time. It was a similar feeling to wandering around the shops when I was waiting at an airport terminal for my flight.

In the chemo ward waiting room there was zero phone signal and no Wi-Fi connection. Nas, Dad and I all waited in silence. Dad was resting his bald head on the back of his plastic chair, looking up to the ceiling, Nas was people watching and I was flicking through the array of leaflets available. I wasn't sure they were making me feel any more at ease. I flicked through the pages of the leaflet titled *Finding the NEW YOU After Cancer*, but I wasn't ready for that. I glanced at the front cover of *Your Sex Life and Cancer*, but not wanting Dad or Nas to see it, I left it alone. My eyes moved down to another leaflet titled *Dying Matters, My Funeral Wishes*. Thankfully, Dr. Wheater finally called us through to his room.

The room didn't exactly scream happiness. The walls were beige, the chairs black and the lighting low. It was the opposite to my dentist's room which was full of light with cool, funky pictures on the ceiling to look at. Dr. Wheater's room was emotionless but perhaps he'd done that on purpose. I liked to think he wore brightly coloured socks or silk patterned pants so his internal extrovert could scream out, 'I'm a fun guy really!' I guessed his office was not always the time or place for happiness. It would be a tad strange to walk in for cancer news and be greeted by photos of Caribbean beaches, or his family skiing trip. It would come across as some sort of morbid gameshow of photos like, 'Here's what you could have won.'

Dr. Wheater offered us a seat in his dull office and discussed the usual procedures. As the patient I always sat adjacent to him, and Nas and Dad would sit on plastic chairs against the wall as if watching a chat show host and their guest. He sat on the edge of his chair and explained that my blood test results were strong enough to have this round of chemotherapy and then asked if I wanted to know my AFP and HCG tumour markers.

I'd heard doctors talk about tumour markers, but I'd never understood or took any notice of what they actually meant. I just thought it was red blood cells and white blood cells. Red blood cells are needed to take oxygen around your body and white blood cells are needed to fight off disease. But HCG and AFP were hormones detected in the blood. HCG was the hormone indicator that Dr. Amafoa joked about before my surgery in relation to me being pregnant. HCG stands for Human Chorionic Gonadotrophin. Ahh, the old gonads. Haven't heard them called that for years. AFP stands for Alpha-Fetoprotein and can also be detected in pregnant women but via a blood test. I remembered this one because AFP was like Af P., my name and initials. My very own hormone named after me. Nas was a lot more knowledgeable about both, so thankfully spoke in my place.

'Ooo, do you have the tumour marker numbers there?' She sat upright on the end of her chair.

'Yes, we have the HCG and AFP results, but it all depends if Afsheen would like to know them or not.' Dr. Wheater addressed my sister in the cheap seats.

'I don't really know what they are to be honest, but ok,' I said. I probably should have known seeing as it was my seventh week of chemo but I'd felt like I was just the vessel, just the body. *It doesn't matter what information I know, just plug me in and get it sorted.*

But Dr. Wheater explained more. 'There are two tumour markers that we test for in your blood count before we do any CT scans. The AFP marker and the HCG hormone, which is the one that pregnant women have.'

'Right, I know about the pregnancy one.'

'Now, the AFP tumour marker should be between ten and twenty.'

'I'm with you so far.'

'When you first came, your AFP was seven hundred and thirty six.'

'Sheesh, that's not very close to ten and twenty.'

'No, but at the start of your second cycle of chemo it had halved to three hundred and forty two, and this week it's down to fifty four.'

'That's good.' I half-heartedly shrugged.

'And your HCG hormone, the one that shows you're pregnant, should be between 0.1 and 0.5.'

'I'm listening.' I sat there, poised, like I was watching the lottery balls roll in.

'In week one your HCG was eight hundred and ninety five, in cycle two it was three hundred and fifty eight and now it's seventy two.'

'Wow, that sounds good.' I still didn't have a clue what any of it really meant, but less than one hundred sounded better than eight hundred and ninety five, that was for sure.

'YES!' Nas screeched and smiled cheek to cheek like I'd never seen before.

I looked to Dad and he stared back with an expression that conveyed he didn't know what was going on either, and then raised a gentle smile anyway. It sounded positive. But I was about to start chemo in an hour followed by another three night stay on the inpatients ward.

Nas, Dad and I left Dr. Wheater's office and went on the hunt for lunch as they'd both suddenly got their appetite back. We were outside the front of the Marks and Spencer in the busiest corridor of the hospital and Nas turned to face me with tears rolling down her face.

'YOU'VE DONE IT!'

'Done what?' I looked around and noticed everyone staring at me.

'YOU'VE BEATEN IT!'

'Have I?'

'YES! Yes, your markers are below one hundred!' Nas grabbed me by both arms and pulled me in for a hug.

'AHHHHH FUCKING HELL!' I shouted, causing people to stare at both of us.

'What, what?' Nas pulled away, concerned.

'My fucking needle mark! They just took the blood out of my arm and you grabbed me by it.'

'Oh, shut up. That's the least of your worries. You've done it!'

Nas was in tears. Happy tears. But I had no feelings. It sounded like good news, but I knew I was about to start chemo and was in for another shitfest. What if I got an irregular heartbeat again? What about the disgusting taste that stayed in my mouth, the sickness, the bloating, the not sleeping, the old man shouting out in the bed opposite all night, the painful injections to my stomach, the cannulas, the heart burn, the indigestion, the feeling of death? For me it wasn't over yet. I could sense a finish line, but I knew I had to run through the proverbial wall one more time.

We slowly walked up the stairs to the chemo ward on the fourth floor. I wondered, *Who will be in the same room as me? Will I have a window bed? Will the anti-sickness tablets work?* It was like walking the green mile to be summoned once more.

After an hour of being in my new hospital bed, Dad and Nas left me and Mum arrived to fill in the late shift. Michelle Parker, an old university friend, had also planned to visit me as she lived locally in Southampton. Michelle and I had met on a night out at university. We'd had a great laugh, added each other on Facebook and in my eyes, she was the number one girl at the University of Brighton. With blonde hair and green eyes, she was short, athletic and played centre for the Netball team. She'd done her university placement year as a physiotherapist at Southampton Hospital, so knew the building well.

Before Michelle arrived, I realised we'd not spoken in person for at least six years. *Will it be awkward? Will we have things to talk about?* I worried.

Michelle skipped into the ward and sat on the plastic chair next to my bed, her face as radiant as ever. She was familiar with the hospital environment and caring for patients. As the nurse inserted a cannula into the top of my wrist, Michelle looked on intently, whereas I was looking the opposite direction trying not to cry. I couldn't use my meditation techniques with Michelle watching by my side. As if I wasn't embarrassed enough, she even offered to empty my bottles of piss that had mounted up on the side table, and waited outside the curtains whilst I filled them up again. Any awkward tension about not seeing each other for six years was forgotten as soon as she emptied a bottle of my urine down a toilet.

Mum left us alone and went to the Macmillan Cancer centre for another manicure from the volunteers. Michelle and I spoke about my cancer, our university days and what she was up to now. We chatted like we were long lost friends. She'd met a new guy – an ex-marine. I wasn't an ex-marine, I was a cancer patient hooked up to an IV drip. The things I would have done to go on a date with Michelle Parker at university and this is what it had come down to. I told Michelle all about the Olympics, Brazil and Luci.

'Have you asked her to come to England?' Michelle said, without an ounce of jealousy.

'Nah, I think it's a bit far and I wouldn't be much fun.'

'Well, why don't you ask her to come when you finish treatment? She might be the perfect distraction.'

'Ahh, she's probably busy with studying.'

'Af, if you don't ask, you'll never know. Just ask.'

I thought about my new mindset, that life was too short. *Why have I never just asked the question? Why do we never ask questions for fear of rejection? Should I have asked Michelle to go on a date at uni? Maybe that's what she was really insinuating.*

Before I had time to process any more of life's questions, the first two hours of my saline drip finished. The first bag of Bleomycin chemo was hooked up to my machine and started trickling into my veins. I could feel the energy vanishing from my body.

'It's like a slow and painful death,' I said. 'Sorry, but I think I'm going to be rubbish now.'

I moved from my upright sitting position and slid my back down the pillows so that I was lying horizontally. My speech started to slow, and I knew the feeling would last for at least the next three days. Michelle moved closer and held my hand. *I'm holding hands with Michelle Parker! This totally counts.* I raised a smile and closed my eyes. Michelle put her other hand on my face and stroked her thumb across my forehead. It was the most relaxing forehead thumb stroke that I'd ever had. Of course, it was. IT WAS MICHELLE PARKER!

I'm not even sure how long Michelle stayed, but I was totally relaxed for once. If there's one way to make chemo bearable, it's your school or university crush holding your hand and stroking your forehead. As I drifted towards sleep, Michelle left the ward, giving Mum a big hug on the way out as if they were two footballers swapping places in a substitution.

'You have lots of nice friends that look out for you, Af.' Mum sat down with her shiny new fingernails from the Macmillan manicure on show.

I woke up the next day to a photo of Rich, George and Dave. They were in Milan to watch Southampton play in the Europa League. It was possibly the biggest game in Southampton's recent years, certainly in my lifetime. We

214

were playing Italian giants Inter Milan at the iconic San Siro Stadium. I'd even bought a ticket with the lads with the intention I could make it. The four of us always travelled to watch Southampton play, even if it was long distances against smaller clubs like Bolton Wanderers, Sheffield Wednesday or Manchester United.

I was gutted to miss the opportunity as Southampton had never played in Europe. Rich had travelled to Italy in a pair of shorts because he thought it would still be hot, even in November. In the photo they sent me he was wearing a black arm band out of respect for my absence. George said Rich had even held a minute's silence before the game for me. I knew I'd never get the opportunity again, but my health came first. I wasn't going to let other opportunities pass me by as soon as I was healthy again though – if I could wait that long.

26.   The Final Bell

Life Lesson: Never celebrate too early.
Cancer Lesson: Take your time.
Song Choice: *The Final Countdown* – Europe

This is it. The home stretch. The last hurdle. You're into injury time and this is the final bell. You might start planning a party. You might think about what you'll do after your final consultation – what meal to treat yourself to and which beer to wash it down with. Yeah, and why not? You've broken the back of chemotherapy; your blood markers are coming down and you have a date set for the final CT Scan.

However, this is where I have to drop this in… caution, caution, caution!

Cancer is just a motherfucker, and you never know what party plans it's going to ruin. It's not uncommon for blood markers to go down as the chemo works, and then as the cancer begins to resist the drugs and blood makers to start going back up again. But positivity is a beautiful tool and keeping the mind stimulated can act as a great distraction.

The week I found out I had cancer was the worst seven days of my life. So, I was determined to walk out the other side of all the shit with some positive memories, and in control. Ask friends and family to join you in creating positive lasting memories. If you're feeling strong enough, I'd suggest making plans for your last week of chemotherapy. But take it easy – don't make plans that require too much exertion. Don't be a fucking idiot. Don't ruin all the hard work. Not now. You've come too far.

I was the idiot.

I reached out to friends to see who was available for my final week of treatment. I only had thirty minutes of chemo planned for the Thursday afternoon, so I scheduled activities for the other days of the week.

On Monday 5th December 2016 the start of my ninth week of chemo, my amazing university friends, Jo and Sam, drove four hours from Kent to visit, and we went skiing at a nearby dry ski-slope. The downhill was great fun, although there were no thrill-seeking parallel slalom turns, just very cautious snow ploughing.

However, the drag lifts up the slope drained all of the energy from my thighs. I was exhausted. Perhaps not the smartest activity during my ninth week of chemotherapy, especially as my last dose had been just four days ago. We should have just gone for a coffee and a walk.

Don't go skiing on a dry-slope during cancer treatment people. Not even if there is a chairlift.

On Tuesday, my long-time friend Nick asked if I'd travel with him to Bristol, two hours away, to pick up some equipment for his gym. I said I'd come for the journey and we ended up going indoor go-karting. I'd been go-karting before and had an 'If you're not first, you're last' attitude. I'd skid around corners sometimes crashing hard into the tyre barriers. But not this time. I drove more like Miss Daisy than Lewis Hamilton. At one point, another driver cut me up on a corner and overtook me. Inside my helmet I shouted, 'I've got fucking cancer, you twat!' They'd already whizzed around the next corner leaving me in their dust as I ranted. It wasn't her fault though; she was only twelve.

Again, not the smartest activity during week nine of chemotherapy treatment. I didn't even make a podium finish, but at least I didn't come last. The thing that made it worse was that the vibrations from the steering wheel had set off the numbness in my hands and I couldn't feel my fingers anymore. It was like I had pins and needles from my fingertips to my elbows. The peripheral neuropathy (numbness of the hands) had been set to level one thousand and it was that bad I had to ask Nick to unscrew the bottle cap from my drink.

On the way home, Nick stopped off to collect the gym equipment we'd come for and asked me to help him lift it into the back of his van. I took one look at my throbbing hands and raised them up to show Nick. They had doubled in size; I had hands like The Hulk. I got out anyway and helped load two one-kilogram weights and a yoga mat into the back of the van.

The man selling the equipment asked why I wasn't helping and I said I had cancer. He was mortified, like I was making some sick joke to get out of the heavy lifting. I had to remove my woolly hat to show him I was actually bald. He looked slightly embarrassed but equally confused as I was still wearing my participation medal from the go-karting track. I quickly got back in the van as they loaded the heavier weights and a full Smith machine. I couldn't even get my phone out of my pocket to scroll because I wouldn't be able to hold it and I didn't know if my new large hands would even fit in my pocket.

Thanks for the day out, Nick, but manual labour was not for me.

Wednesday was golf day. My friend Will had driven from Essex as he'd arranged a work meeting in Dorset just so that he could skive off early and play nine holes of golf with me. Will plays three times a week and is a far better golfer than I am. He's a true east Londoner who loves nothing more than West Ham and Stella Artois. When he's not in his golf attire, he's dripping in Barbour clothing and a flat cap, and usually shouting, 'Irons!'

Will was straight off the bat with the testicle jokes. As I lined up my shot on the first tee he said, 'Don't lose that ball, you've only got one.' A few holes later when I actually lost a ball in the bushes, he followed with, 'It's not like you to lose a ball.'

Now, I'm not sure if Will did this on purpose to make me feel better, but he scuffed a shot off the sixth tee that made the ball go five yards in front of him. It was the biggest mis-hit I've ever seen in my life from a proper golfer, and I fell on the floor dying of laughter. It couldn't have happened to a better bloke. He was certainly more forgiving with me than Rich had been at Badminton. He was giving me putts within five feet. I won that round of golf, but Will always claims that he let me win that day.

Golf was a good choice. I still wasn't great, but at least it didn't leave me in pain the way skiing and go-karting had.

After three days of Af's adventures, I really did appreciate the lengths people had gone to spend time with me. Friends had driven two, three, four hours to hang out, and it was mid-week too. Before cancer, I didn't see friends who live twenty minutes away. Equally my fault. My phone was always full of messages and missed calls.

It really made me think about how much time we give each other. We can all become so wrapped up in our lives and our own little bubbles that next thing you know, you haven't seen someone for five years. I've been one of those people who doesn't send a text because they're too 'busy'. Cancer was proving to me that we could always make time for each other, and having those connections are so fulfilling because at the end of the day, the most valuable thing someone can give you is their time. That and to play some poor golf shots in a competition with you.

I'd had such a fun-filled three days that I hadn't even thought about my upcoming chemotherapy session. My final session on Thursday now felt like a total inconvenience. It was taking time away from my busy skiing, go-karting and golfing schedule.

Dad took me to Dorset County Hospital, and we checked in as usual. The new consultant, who I'd never met before, checked my records and was thrilled that my blood counts were showing decreasing signs of the tumour markers. She was a lot happier than any other consultant I'd seen in my entire cancer journey, which filled me with confidence and put me at ease even more. However, after another blood test, the positively happy consultant called Dad and me into her office one more time.

'Look, your blood markers have improved, so your body is responding to the chemotherapy, which is amazing.'

'That's great news,' I replied, interacting with much more energy than I had done with my consultants at Poole and Southampton Hospitals.

'Yes, but your white blood cell count is dangerously low, and your immune system is at risk at the moment, so you'll have to stay home for a week and screen yourself away from visitors. Ok?'

'A week?' I blurted out.

'Yes, It's just one more week. The time will go quickly, don't worry.'

'I can't stay home for a week.'

'Why not?'

'I've got tickets to Anthony Joshua's boxing match in Manchester on Saturday. Eddie Hearn gave me them for free. I've got the train booked.'

'How many people will be at the fight?'

'It's a sold-out arena so probably twenty thousand.'

'WHAT! At a boxing match? You absolutely cannot go to an event that big and risk picking up an infection. Not at this stage. You need to stay at home and rest. One more week and then you can start your life again.'

'One more week to wait, yeah?'

Dad and I went back to the waiting area of the chemotherapy ward for my number to be called. Dorset County Hospital is on a smaller scale to Poole and Southampton, especially the chemotherapy ward for day visitors. I sat there with not a strand of hair on my head or body. I was gaunt and looking exactly like a cancer victim. Everyone else had either a full head of hair or they were wearing some impressive wigs. I didn't want to brag but I looked like I had gone through the mill compared to everyone else. As I looked down at my hospital wristband that had my name and date of birth on it, I was called to a chemotherapy room. Dad stayed in the waiting room as he'd fallen asleep. I was totally fine with that. He had continued to work hard on his business, had shaved his hair completely off like mine, and he was doing everything for me. Just like everyone else, he had really stepped up to the plate since my asthma attack. He must have been exhausted so I went and had the last bout of chemo on my own.

Most chemotherapy wards have something special in them and that is a bell. A big shiny bell to ring once you've had your last chemotherapy session. It gives you and everyone hope and something to aim for. It's emotional watching someone walk towards that bell and ring it. It's more than just a bell, it's a symbol of getting closer to freedom. I had eyed up the bell in Southampton and Poole hospitals, but I'd be ringing the bell hard in Dorchester.

I came out of my last chemotherapy session and looked over at Dad who was still silently sleeping in the waiting room chair with his fingers interlocked across his chest. I grabbed the rope at the bottom of the bell, looked at Dad again and thought, *FUCK IT!* I rang that damn bell so hard that people will have heard it down the road. Dad jumped out of his skin, knocking his phone onto the floor. He gave me a startled look of annoyance, but I couldn't stop laughing. Rather than being upset that I had suffered through it all, I was crying laughter tears as the rest of the waiting room laughed at my wickedness. Sorry, Dad. Chemo was over!

On Friday, I stayed at home, resting in bed and self-isolating as per the doctor's instructions.

Saturday, I boarded the 8:57am train from Weymouth to London and met up with university friends at London Bridge for our annual Christmas dinner get together. It was slightly awkward as some were seeing me for the first time bald as badger. This was when John handed me a 'testicle' as my secret Santa gift – an avocado stone in a jar of apple cider vinegar. It was incredibly lifelike, and it stayed in the jar on the table whilst everyone ate their Christmas turkey.

My friend Turton and I tubed to London St Pancras to catch the 2:04pm train to Manchester Piccadilly, but not before I had to go to the ticket office to explain that I'd lost all of my hair and eyebrows due to treatment, which was why I looked nothing like my photo on my railcard.

Turton and I had travelled across the UK and Europe a lot for different sporting events. Turton's mum passed away after suffering with a brain tumour so, unfortunately, looking after sick people was nothing new to him. The day would have been tiring for anyone, but I still had chemo drugs coursing through me from two days previously. I tried to nap on the train, in between Turton waking me up to point at things outside the window.

I'd been to boxing events all my life. I'd boxed myself from the age of twelve to twenty, before going into event management and working internationally. I'd probably watched over three thousand boxing matches live, but the fights in the big arenas are totally different occasions.

We arrived early at the Manchester Arena as we wanted to watch the undercard fights before Anthony Joshua's world championship title main event. I went to the toilets and every cubicle had cigarette smoke floating above its door. As the night went on, the men just smoked at the urinals. A bloke pissed out of his head walked in holding his crotch. He waited for a urinal to become free and said, 'Has anyone got a spare cigarette?' A geezer pissing in the urinal next to me had his hand up against the wall while puffing on a fag hanging out the side of his mouth. He turned around without any hesitation and replied, 'Sorry mate, you can't smoke in here.'

I was completely sober, surrounded by twenty thousand drunk people, with the groggiest feeling in my head and cigarette smoke stinging my eyes, but I still had to laugh at that. British humour at its finest. The other testosterone-fuelled men joined in and laughed at the joke too.

Turton and I settled down into our seats, in the first row of the lower balcony. The raised height offered the perfect view. I couldn't believe my luck. 'Thank you, Eddie Hearn,' I shouted. All the seats around us were empty as people were still at the bars or smoking in the toilets.

As the night went on, more people came and sat down in their seats. There was a perfect correlation – the later someone arrived to their seat, the drunker they were. As each fight started, the stands filled with more people than the previous fight, apart from the three seats to the left of me. The fight just before the main event had just finished; a twelve-round brawl between Dillian Whyte and Derek Chisora. It had been edge of your seat stuff and a candidate for fight of the year.

Finally, the empty seats beside me were taken up by three lads just before Anthony Joshua's fight was about to begin. They were the drunkest men in Manchester. *Why does everything really good have to have a little bit of shit with it just to balance it out? It always has to be Ying and Yang.* I tried to ignore their drunkenness and focus on the atmosphere building in the boxing ring as Neil Diamond's *Sweet Caroline* rang through the arena. The drunk lads all wanted to shake my hand and be friends with everyone. Usually this would have been fine, but I had a low immune system and I didn't know where their hands had been.

The stadium lights went out and Manchester Arena was plunged into darkness. Anthony Joshua's entrance music came on, accompanied by a video of him on the jumbo screen above the ring. He walked in slowly to the music of Nas (the rapper, not my sister), flames igniting from either side of him. The atmosphere in the arena was electric.

The MC Michael Buffer excited the crowd with, 'Let's get readyyy to rumbleeeeee!' and one of the drunkest men in Manchester spilt his beer over my knee.

This is payback for every sober person I've ever annoyed whilst being drunk, I thought.

The fight started and as soon as the first bell went 'ding ding', the man next to me went to the toilets. *Maybe he came just to see the ring walk? Maybe he needs another line of coke?* But it meant I could relax and watch the fight without him leaning on me. Two minutes into the second round, Anthony Joshua's opponent Eric Molina was laid out on the canvas in the same position I'd been lying in during chemo in my hospital bed. The drunkest man in Manchester had missed the entire five minutes of the fight.

It had been a pretty epic week in terms of excitement and fun, but I was all out of fun by that point. I was exhausted. The skiing had killed my legs, the go-karting had killed my hands, and the boxing match would have been great to watch on the TV. It had been a good week of distractions but maybe a puzzle or some Lego would have been more appropriate.

However, I had one more day of excitement to come…

On Sunday, I drove to London Heathrow Airport to meet Luci at the arrivals gate of Terminal 3.

27. Luci In The Sky

Life Lesson: Say yes.
Cancer Lesson: There is no rule book.
Song Choice: *Lucy in the Sky With Diamonds* – The Beatles

Throughout this book, I've tried to make my advice and stories relatable in the hope of helping to make your cancer journey easier. I'm not sure how relatable I can make this next bit, but let's go with it anyway.

On Sunday 11th December 2016, the day before I was booked into Southampton Hospital for my final CT Scan, blood tests and THE cancer results, Luci was arriving in the UK from Brazil. As if getting cancer results wasn't surreal enough, I thought I'd add a little Brazilian spice into the mix.

Luci had never travelled out of Brazil before in her life. She'd never felt a temperature lower than 10°C. Luci didn't own a coat. She landed at London Heathrow Airport at 4pm. It was 3° and due to get colder.

I waited in the arrivals section of the airport with a bunch of flowers, like the romantics do. I'd been tracking her flight on the internet for the eleven-hour journey and knew that her plane had landed safely. Two hours had passed since her flight had landed and there was still no sight of her. As the minutes turned to hours, every scenario crossed my mind. *Did she actually get on the plane in Brazil? Was she having visa problems at customs? Has she seen my new bald fat head and walked straight back to the departures lounge?*

I watched every single person come through the automatic doors and tried to guess where they had arrived from. The arrivals terminal at Christmas is more exciting than the rest of the year. The usual business suits walked through the doors and straight to their waiting executive taxi drivers, but there were the Christmas holiday passengers too, reuniting with excited friends and family. But people were now walking through in big coats too. *These surely haven't flown from Rio*, I thought.

I tried calling Luci and sending her messages, but nothing was going through. *She could have joined the airport Wi-Fi and sent me a message by now?* After what felt like the five-hundredth time, the arrival doors opened again and Luci came bouncing through. She gave me the best hug that only she could do, hugging me so tightly as her bright white teeth chattered with cold shivers. She was wearing a new goofy pair of glasses, but her smile had lit up my world again. We hadn't seen each other in over thirteen weeks but it felt like a lifetime. A lot had changed in a short time. Physically and mentally, I looked and felt completely different due to obvious reasons, and Luci was not in Rio, or on the beach, and she was cold!

'What took you so long? I thought you didn't get on the plane.' I gave Luci my coat to try and warm her up.

'They searched my bags… for this.' She pulled a big bag of white powder out of her backpack.

'What the hell is that?'

'It's Farofa, we use it to cook in Brazil, I wanted to make you some Brazilian food.'

'It looks like cocaine, and you had that in your hand luggage?' I nervously laughed.

'Yes, the man in customs tasted it.'

'No wonder you took so long, he thought you were a drugs mule.'

'Yes, but the real cocaine is hidden in my shampoo bottle.'

'Luci!'

'Calma baby, it's a joke, let's go to home,' she said.

Luci Escobar and I walked through the airport and paid for the extortionate London Heathrow parking. As soon as we walked across the car park, Luci noticed her own breath in the cold air. You know when it's so cold you can see your breath and it looks like smoke? She'd never experienced that in her twenty-five years in Brazil. She couldn't stop laughing at it, and for the first twenty minutes of the car journey, she finished every sentence with an imaginary cigarette in her hand, puffing out fake smoke with her cold breath.

She was soon disorientated as the daytime turned to darkness even though it was only just past 5pm. Luci and her fake cigarette smoking had taken my mind off results day, but she was soon fast asleep for the remaining two hours of the car journey.

When we eventually pulled up outside Mum's, Luci thought the small two-bedroom house was a mansion compared to my Rio apartment. I wasn't expecting Luci to be full of life on our arrival to Mum's house. I know how it feels after a long flight, trying to put on a spritely face for people whilst sitting there with red eyeballs trying to tell them what the plane was like. But as soon as Mum opened the door, Luci jumped on her. She wrapped both arms around her back, screaming, squealing and squeezing Mum like they were long-lost mother and daughter.

'Mummy, Mummy!'

Mum's always been a bit reserved with people and I knew she'd never met anyone from South America before. She definitely wasn't used to this sort of greeting and I stood back and laughed as she melted into Luci's embrace.

Luci walked in, kicked off her shoes and sat down in the armchair like she'd returned home from a long holiday. Mi casa es su casa: my house is your house. Then she inspected all of the Christmas tree decorations like they were made of real gold. I was excited by how excited she was. The Darts World Championships was on the TV. Have you ever tried describing the concept of darts to someone who's never seen it? I tried explaining why fifteen thousand people dressed as vicars, nuns and Where's Wallys would go and watch two large men throw twenty-two grams of tungsten at a board, but even I ended up being confused.

It had been a long day and although Luci's body clock was four hours behind on Brazilian time, she was exhausted, and we soon went to bed. She was out like a light as soon as her head hit the pillow, but I couldn't get my results day off my mind. I sat up in bed with Luci hugging my waist and turned to social media one more time.

8:31pm on 11th December 2016 – Facebook:

So, I wasn't going to make this public, but everyone's been involved in this challenge from the start, so you may as well continue to be on the journey. Tomorrow is judgement day for results. I'll be having scans, blood tests and X-rays throughout the day. I didn't want to tell people for fear of tempting fate or having to cope with the level of disappointment that tomorrow could bring. But it's the support that's got me through everything so far so why change?

Now, I'm not naive enough to think I can positively think myself out of medical science, but I have a favour to ask. If you pray and there's such a thing as praying harder, then get on your knees tonight, close your eyes and really clench those fists. If you have healing crystals, then hold them for a second longer. If you rub Buddha's belly, then give him an extra rub tonight. If you have lucky pants, then get them out in the morning and put them on.

I'll be having a catch up whatever the news, so if you are in Weymouth then please come say hi in Actors bar between 8-10pm (heavy drinkers are encouraged to stay later). Don't be shy and please pop along.

I've been imagining this day for twelve weeks now and it starts tomorrow.

The first day of the rest of my life.

As we come to what could be the end of this adventure, it's a good time to reflect on what it has taught us.

The nerves have not kicked in just yet but tomorrow afternoon is the big time.

What a time to be alive!

28.   So, That's It Then?

Life Lesson: Don't bottle emotions.
Cancer Lesson: There is no finish line.
Song Choice: *Greatest Day* – Take That

The three most anti-climactic moments in my life are losing my virginity, handing in my dissertation, and being told I had the all-clear from cancer. You might wonder, *How can that be?* Getting the all-clear was a feeling unlike any emotion I've ever had before. *Am I supposed to start crying? Start jumping up and down? Or run down the corridors shouting, 'We did it!'?* Now I'm not made of stone. Of course, I felt emotional but where were the dramatics? It was supposed to be like the movies or the soap operas. You see the cancer research adverts of patients getting the all-clear and they all react differently to the news. Some smile with joy, some cry with emotion and some hug the doctors.

I guess a reason for the emotions not immediately pouring out in the consultant's room is because honestly… it's not totally over. It's not like the doctor says, 'You've completed the test, now get on with your life and don't come back.'

There are scans on the screen showing you the size of your cancer and what it has shrunk down to. There's an explanation about your five-year remission plan. The booking of a check-up appointment in just one month's time to make sure the tumour has not started growing again. Growing again? Oh, bloody hell, please don't. An explanation that you'll come back every three months for the first year of your remission, every four months in your second year and then every six months for the following THREE YEARS. Five more years of worrying about this shite, for fuck's sake. At least you get to keep the 'exempt from payment' card for five years for your prescription medication. Always positives. All this new information delays any onset of emotion, but don't worry... it'll come.

Monday 12th December 2016 was a strange day to wake up to. A day that I'd been waiting for yet I had anxiety about nonetheless. Scanxiety. It was the first day of the rest of my life.

I woke up early and Luci was already awake watching Brazilian YouTube dance videos on her phone. We went downstairs where my step-dad, Ian had cooked a full English breakfast.

'Baked beans? For breakfast?' Luci laughed at the alien concoction of sausage, bacon, eggs, mushrooms, tomato, baked beans and fried bread on the plate.

'And the bread is fried?' She held her cup of tea with her pinkie out pretending to be the Queen. If there was one person that could take my mind off the upcoming dread then it was Luci. Her comedy and craziness must have been sent to me by something greater than life itself. A godsend if you will.

Dad arrived at the house to pick up Mum, Luci and I to drive us to Southampton Hospital for my final check-up. I could sense the tension in the car, but boy, was it clean. Dad must have had it valeted and it smelled fresh with a hint of lavender. He even had the *Dogs Smell Cancer* air freshener hooked onto his mirror.

Throughout the journey, conversation was always steered away from any sort of cancer talk. Luci was the perfect distraction and Dad asked her the usual questions about how the flight was and what it was like to live in Brazil. He asked if she'd heard that Weymouth had a carnival which was a bit like Rio carnival (it's not). He drove slowly past Weymouth beach trying to compare it to Copacabana. Luci's English would always suffer when she was tired and she was still a bit dazed from the flight, so the conversation wasn't entirely free flowing.

Nas met us at the hospital and she led the way towards ward C3, with Mum and Dad just behind her and Luci and I at the back. We were in the Mighty Ducks flying 'V' formation. Not on purpose, may I add, but the reason ducks fly in this formation is to support each other from front to back. We were no different. Ducks fly together.

As we walked through the hospital corridors Luci pointed at the queue for the Subway shop.

'Subway Sandwich?' She laughed, reflecting on the first time I was diagnosed with a tumour back in Rio and her first action was to buy me a meatball mariana.

I was due to have blood tests, an X-ray on my chest and an upper-body CT scan. Everything felt like one last goodbye. I walked to the X-ray room and thought of Fred and how he was doing. I wondered if he was still receiving treatment while working and drinking Guinness with ginger. I went to the CT scan room, drunk the dye and felt like I was pissing myself in the machine again. One last goodbye to the Starship Enterprise device made by

Samsung the mobile phone company. I laid in the CT scan machine thinking about how much life had changed since paddle boarding in Rio. *What must Luci be thinking and how is she getting on with my family?*

As I came out from the scan, she was tucking into her first ever roast dinner from the hospital canteen. As I walked to see her and my family, she held up a yorkshire pudding. She'd eaten everything else on the plate and I asked her why she'd left the yorkshire until last.

'It's a pudding, it's dessert no?' she said, breaking the yorkshire pudding with her hands.

I'd wanted to show Luci the sites of Great Britain like Big Ben, Buckingham Palace and the Natural History Museum. Not the inside of Southampton hospital. She really was one of a kind.

I didn't have a chance to see the nurses on ward C3 that had looked after me so many times, but I did manage to say bye to the volunteers in the Macmillan centre. We had a cup of tea in their lounge area and a volunteer gave Mum a hand massage.

Then we all moved to the cancer ward waiting area. I took my ticket for the blood test queue, but before my number was called, Dr. Wheater's office door opened.

'Afsheen… would you like to come through?' he called across the waiting room. *No actually, I wouldn't like to come through, Dr. Wheater.* But it was a rhetorical question so up I got. I felt slightly guilty walking across the waiting room full of cancer patients as I was going in for my results. I was the prisoner walking past my jail mates on my way to see if the parole board would set me free into civilisation. I'm sure they were all happy for me, but they still had more time to serve.

Mum and Dad sat on the two chairs by Dr. Wheater's desk and Nas and Luci stood next to them. I took the singular plastic chair in the direction that Dr. Wheater was facing. I looked up at the clock and it was 3:16pm. I knew I'd remember that time forever. If I was a religious man, I'd have thought it was a sign of God.

John 3:16 – *For God so loved the world, that he gave his only begotten Son, that whosoever believeth in him should not perish, but have eternal life.*

Is this a sign from God? Was it going to be good news? Was I going to have eternal life? I believed in God like I believed in WWE wrestling and my favourite wrestler Stone Cold Steve Austin's catchphrase is, 'Austin 3:16 says I just whooped your ass.' This was the confirmation I needed that I'd kicked cancer's ass before Dr. Wheater had even opened his mouth.

We waited awkwardly for seconds, which felt like minutes, for Dr. Wheater to say something.

'Right, that's it then.' He twiddled his fingers together.

'That's it?' Dad asked before the doctor had a chance to follow up his sentence.

'Yep, all done.' Dr. Wheater brushed it off like he'd just extracted a tooth or something. Had he forgotten that I was bald, lifeless, full of nine weeks of chemo? Where's the drama, Doc? Where's the tension? Build it up, add a little razzamatazz. These are my lottery numbers; this isn't just some routine check-up.

Dr. Wheater swivelled his computer monitor around and showed us his screen.

'This picture on the left is the tumour that you had on your lymph nodes in September, and this scan on the right is you now.' He was doing that thing where to him what he was saying made perfect sense, but to me it was just scans and all I could see was a slight change in the size of something.

We all nodded like we knew exactly what we were looking at.

'We'll see you again next month for some follow up tests. If all is well, then we'll see you every three months for the first year, then every four months for year two, and then every six months for the three years after that.'

I thought I was just going to get on with my life pre-cancer. Not these check-ups and blood tests all the time.

'The cancer has a one in ten chance of returning in the first twelve months of your remission and that will halve each year after that,' Dr. Wheater said with an honest conviction. I was being set free, but I was still on probation. For a crime I didn't commit, may I add.

We all stood up and shook Dr. Wheater's hand and thanked him for everything. I didn't know what else to say to him, but it came out anyway.

'Thank you for everything, Doctor, but in the nicest possible way, I hope I never have to see you ever again.'

Dr. Wheater gave a little chuckle. 'I hope so too, Afsheen.'

We all shuffled out the door in a bit of disbelief. *Right, that's it then.* It was so blasé, but that was his job. Sometimes he delivered good news and sometimes he delivered terrible news. I guessed keeping that emotional disconnection was what was needed for the job.

Mum, Dad, Nas and Luci left the cancer ward and waited outside in the corridor as I went to the phlebotomist's room to have my final blood test.

I walked into the room, took a seat in the oversized blue rubber chair and placed my arm into the arm rest ready for the nurse to start. I'd never seen the nurse before but she was just as friendly, kind and upbeat as all of the nurses I'd come across. She put the tourniquet around my arm whilst looking at my veins and asked for my details one final time.

'What's your full name and date of birth please?'

'Afsheen Panjalizadeh-Marseh, twenty-seventh of the sixth, nineteen eighty-seven.'

'Perrrrfect and are you ok with needles, Afsheen?'

Before I could get any words out, my eyes started to fill with tears.

'Ohh, are you ok, Afsheen? It's only a small scratch, it won't hurt that much.'

I bent over in the chair and started weeping. I couldn't stop the tears as my shoulders heaved up and down. I breathed heavily though my nose and started crying uncontrollably, like a baby. Within the deep breaths and tears rolling down my face, I said, 'I've just... been given... the all-clear.' I put my head onto my arms and cried hysterically, like I've never done before in my life.

The nurse held me and hugged me and started crying too. I looked up and another lady getting her bloods was also crying, and so was the nurse that was taking her bloods. I'm not sure if I had been 'acting strong' throughout my journey to keep everyone together but everything poured out in the space of seconds. We all started laughing and crying. Laughing at how uncontrollable we all were.

The nurse poured me a glass of water and we composed ourselves for her to take my final bloods. For the first time since I found the tumour, all I wanted was my mum. I walked out into the hospital corridor with red watery eyes and Mum grabbed me and hugged me, her tears running onto my shoulder.

We'd done it!

29. Road To Freedom

Life Lesson: It's never too late to try.
Cancer Lesson: Set new goals and take your time.
Song Choice: *Proud* – Heather Small

You've done it! Fuck! Your team has done it. You might think you did it all with your family, friends, and health carers but it couldn't have been done without you. What a fucking journey!

As I stated at the beginning of this challenge, cancer can be the easy part. As a patient, you know what to focus on. It's survival mode. It's game day. Get to your appointments, rest well, take the medication, get plugged into chemo drips, and listen to medical advice. Everything else becomes secondary. The ancient Chinese philosopher Confucius said, 'A healthy man wants a thousand things, a sick man only wants one.' Now hopefully, you will begin to have your health again.

Confucius also said, 'We have two lives; the second begins when we realise we only have one.' I think getting the all-clear from cancer should constitute the beginning of your second life. It's a fresh start, a new outlook and a chance to reinvent yourself.

Your second chance cancer card can make you become the confident person you want to be, and if old friends don't like the new you, you can just blame it on the cancer. Will you become more patient or more assertive? Maybe both. Will you be all-loving and benevolent or more reclusive and precious about your own time and well-being? You'll figure it out I'm sure. But one thing is certain: this is a new you. That might be difficult to accept in your early remission years, but being aware of changes will help that process.

If you're reading this as you get the all-clear, I urge you to celebrate. The day you get the all-clear will become your cancerversary. The weeks leading up to your one-year cancerversary can be quite significant and you might end up celebrating it more than your actual birthday. A cancerversary cake. Bet you never thought you'd be having one of those. If you're not overly keen on cancerversary cakes, maybe book in something adrenaline fuelled instead, like jumping out of a plane for a sky dive. I was fine with the cake.

Of course, it is a time to be happy, however, there is a need to understand the troubles of remission that will creep up on you as time goes by. The anxiety of the follow-up appointments and the niggles and pains that make you think, *Is it back?* The phone stops ringing and the supportive friends stop texting back as much. The friends that disappeared through your treatment return like nothing happened. And the hair. The hair that takes a lot longer than you think to grow back, making you still look like a victim months down the line.

But now, it is time to celebrate. Celebrate with your family and close friends. It's a chance for you to shout out on social media too. Make it a good status or post because it will get you record likes and is a chance to say thank you to all the people that supported you.

Mum, Dad, Nas, Luci, and I left Southampton Hospital for the final time. It had been a wonderful caring place but hopefully we would never see it again. Nas collected the 'free parking' passes from reception that we'd been given due to me being a cancer patient, and we headed back to the car park.

We reached the car and Nas opened the boot. She had brought a bottle of champagne and five plastic champagne flutes.

'Who wants a glass?' She poured the champagne and handed out flutes to us all.

We all charged them and waited for someone to start the cheers.

'What shall we cheers to?' I watched the bubbles rise to the top of the plastic cup.

'To cancer,' Dad blurted out.

'Umm, no. How about… to freedom.' Nas raised her drink.

'To family.' Luci tried to clink her plastic cup with everyone else's plastic cup.

We all discreetly sipped the small champagne servings as Nas felt guilty for drinking it in a hospital car park.

'It might make people feel sad, like we're rubbing it in their faces.' She hid the bottle in the boot of the car like illegal contraband.

'Yes, or it could make people happy that there's light at the end of the tunnel.' Mum looked to the bottom of her now empty cup.

We had a quick photo opportunity with our blue *You Got This* wristbands lifted aloft before piling back into Dad's car.

Dad drove us back to Weymouth in his Mercedes, and I started arranging for friends to come to his bar for some celebratory drinks that evening. I could hear conversations going on in the car, but I just wanted to tell my friends the good news. It had gone 4pm and I'd not posted anything or texted anyone and the longer I took, the more they might start to worry.

I'd had three missed calls from John, so I called him back. He was elated. I then replied to James in Australia and he sent me a selfie of him crying with tears running down his cheeks, saying how proud he was. Real men, showing real emotions. I texted my old boss from Essex who had originally sent me a good luck card saying *Just another challenge* with a reply saying *Challenge complete, what next?* I sent a 'send too many' message on WhatsApp to all of my supporters and friends saying *This is the greatest day of my life so far*. They all sent their amazing congratulations, but there was one message I still had to send that meant the most.

I had to let Julian know the good news and thank him for all the support he'd shown me. I knew everyone would be happy to hear I'd got the all-clear, but they hadn't known the true struggles of what it really meant to face cancer. Julian was still undergoing chemotherapy and visiting University College London for a new Ewing's Sarcoma trial drug. Everyone on this journey had shown weaknesses at some point – either denial, emotion, anger or avoidance. But Julian had been my rock and voice of reason throughout. The one person I could talk to who would give me the truth. We'd hung out walking the dogs, recorded vlogs together and texted each other whilst having baths in the evenings. I wanted to let Julian know the good news and, more importantly, that I couldn't have done the journey without him.

Af: *Mate, I got the all-clear. I couldn't have done it without you, brother. Now it's my turn to be here for you. We got this!*

Julian: *The BEST NEWS! You smashed it. So happy for you.*

Many cancer survivors can go through post-traumatic stress disorder (PTSD) or survivor's guilt. Thanks to the support Julian had given me, I knew I would always be able to pay it forward to anyone else who needed support too.

Once I'd let my close family and friends know the good news I took to Facebook once more…

5.15pm on 12ᵗʰ December 2016 – Facebook:

The greatest day of my life!
The doctor told us just after 3pm today that I am cancer free and have got the all-clear.
After surgery to remove a testicle and nine weeks and fifteen sessions of gruelling chemotherapy. I know you might think it's flown by, but living with it twenty-four-seven, it didn't go as quick.

I can't thank everyone enough that has been involved in this chapter. Literally everyone that has sent me good luck messages.

Hopefully you'll accept this news as my Christmas gift to you all, but it will never match you being part of saving my life.

I can't put into words these feelings and emotions, but what a time to be alive!

Today is first day of the rest of my life.

There's always a message behind every challenge and adventure you go through, but if you take anything away from this episode, I want you to remember one thing... YOU GOT THIS!!!!!!!!!

The greatest day of my life, so far.

We did it and I love you all.

Af xxx

We soon got home and relaxed before the evening ahead. I felt quite empty even though I'd just been given the all-clear. It was a kind of nothingness inside me, like all the adrenaline had vanished. For the past four months, I'd known what my daily life consisted of, which was beating this shit. Maybe it was a case of Paradise Syndrome and a *What now?* uncertainty.

Mum came upstairs to my room holding her phone out to me. Grandma and Grandad were on video call on their iPad. Grandma was so happy for me and said how proud she was about how I'd approached the last few months. Grandad was ecstatic and asked when I'd be over to record some more video blogs with him because he'd written some new stories, jokes and songs to share. They both held up a glass of Bucks Fizz to the camera and said cheers to good health.

Luci, Mum, Ian and I all got ready for the night and in true Brazilian style, we were late to the party. Friends had arrived at Dad's bar around 8pm and started texting me asking where I was as it was now getting closer to 8.30pm.

I had no idea how many people would actually attend as a result of my invite for a Monday night drink. Mum and Ian entered the bar first and Luci and I walked in nervously at the back. There were about forty friends all chatting and drinking. A small group at the bar spotted me walking in and stopped talking. Then everyone went silent and turned in my direction. The background chatter stopped and the only sound was music on a low volume. Before I had a chance to say hello or wave to anyone, Rich started a slow clap round of applause, and was soon joined by everyone else. The whole bar was clapping for me. I didn't know what to do so I just stood there and smiled. I'd always wanted attention, but not like this. I'd done some cool things in my life, that could have been celebrated, but not cancer.

The friends that I'd expected to be there were all there, but I also saw unexpected guests like a former colleague who was now working on a local radio station. Another friend, Ros, who I'd worked with in Rio had driven two hours from Bristol to be there. I felt like Del Boy when he and Rodney walked into the Nag's Head after they'd finally become millionaires.

'Right, what you drinking?' Rich shouted across the bar as he held out his credit card to the bar staff.

'I'll have a beer and Luci would like one too please.'

'A pint for baldy and the Brazilian please.' Rich pointed to the draft pumps.

Everyone soon went back to their group conversations and a bit of normality resumed. I took a sip of my first pint of lager in four months and tried my best not to grimace in front of anyone. The taste was vile. *How can people like this?* It was like that first time you try a sip of your dad's beer as a young child. Disgusting!

As the night went on, I had conversations with small groups of friends and thanked them for coming. I couldn't stand the beer so tried a vodka and Coke. That was equally as revolting. I was soon on just Diet Coke but told people it had vodka in it. I had the quick realisation that I wasn't totally recovered yet, but people wanted the old Af back instantly. None more so than Rich, of course.

Dad had booked a Madness tribute band to play as I'd told him I loved the song *One Step Beyond* about ten years previously. In the interval, Rich grabbed the mic and started his own Karaoke session. He was very drunk but hilarious and everyone paid attention to drunk Rich singing *Back For Good* by Take That. Not to be outdone, Luci joined him on another microphone to do backing vocals. She didn't know the words but filled the gaps between lyrics with 'ooohs' and 'ahhhs'. It completely took the attention away from me, and I was very happy about that.

Later, Luci and I were at the bar again when Dad came over to talk with us.

'So, where are you taking our Brazilian guest this week?' Dad clinked his glass against ours.

'We're not sure yet, maybe the New Forest and a day out in London to see Buckingham Palace at least.'

'Do you like Paris?' Dad asked Luci.

'My dream,' she replied, her eyes melting.

'Well make sure you see the Eiffel Tower at night time when it's all lit up. I've booked you both the Eurostar and a hotel by the Arc de Triomphe.' Dad put a bunch of folded-up pieces of paper into her hand with *Booking.com* written across the top.

'THE CITY OF LOVEEEEE!' Luci jumped up and wrapped both her legs around my dad's waist, causing him to lose his balance and fall back onto the pillar behind. She then went to jump on me but knew I was still too weak for those kinds of celebrations, so just hugged me and kissed me on the lips instead.

The Madness tribute band started playing again after their interval. We were all entertained by Luci trying to teach everyone to dance Samba to renditions of *Baggy Trousers* and *Our House*.

Soon after, people started to drift off home as it was a Monday night, and I was glad the party wasn't going to go into the early hours. I was completely spent of energy. It had been an adventure but one that I didn't want to do again.

Three days later, I got to take Luci to see Buckingham Palace and we travelled on the Eurostar to Paris. Exactly one week after my all-clear announcement we toasted with Champagne, in a proper glass, at the top of the Eiffel Tower. We spent Christmas day together with my extended family and she flew back to Rio on the 30th December. It was an emotional drawn-out goodbye at Heathrow Airport, not knowing when or if we'd ever see each other again. We'd only signed up to a foreign language's website for some fun, but here we were six months down the line – falling in love, beating cancer and seeing Europe.

You never know what or who is waiting around the corner to shake up your world. Luci certainly had done that to mine.

The truth about cancer is that it doesn't end with the all-clear date. Remission is equally as tough. Especially mentally. It becomes more difficult to talk about cancer, but the emotions still play on your mind. I'd advise you to join some cancer communities and dip in and out of them when you feel the need. And remember to take care of yourself and other cancer survivors, even when you think they've reached the finish line.

I'd finally reached my finish line and I was ready for my five-year remission plan and to find the new me. *Maybe I'll write a book about it one day.*

Final Thoughts

As I started this book saying you get a lot of questions during a new cancer diagnosis. They also continue past the all-clear. There's the obvious 'Are you ok now?' but you'll probably also get asked many times, 'Do you think cancer changed you?' The short answer, Yes. Of course it changed me. But all life experiences change you, develop you, make you learn about yourself. Did cancer speed up the process for me to change as a person? Probably, but who knows. Growing older changes you, learning to drive, having children, falling in love. Life is for learning. In terms of did it change me as a person. I find joy in so many hidden places that I didn't know before. My dogs, warm rain, grass between my toes. The little joys of life. I know I was incredibly privileged to receive some of the support that I did. I also know that some are not as fortunate to receive the all-clear from cancer. Hopefully if we keep talking about it we can find more treatments and cures much sooner.

My life had kind of prepared me for a challenge as great as cancer. I had always voluntarily put myself outside of my comfort zone. When you face challenges that really scare you and intimidate you, that's where you find out about yourself,. When you're running through the proverbial wall at mile nineteen of a marathon, that's when you go to the dark places in your head, but when you complete mile twenty-six, you realise your full potential.

I didn't sign up to all my challenges and adventures thinking that they might stand me in good stead to beat cancer one day. I signed up to them because I wanted to be able to achieve everyday life goals, such as talking to people or having confidence in my abilities. Like many, I had crippling shyness, even around my own family, but I thought, *If I can run a marathon, surely I can say hello to someone, or hold a conversation without having heart palpitations. Maybe I'll even have something interesting to talk about at parties.* I hated elements of the boxing matches, the mountain climbing, the long distance cycling, appearing on *The Chase* TV game show and the stand-up comedy to the point of physical sickness, but each event taught me something new about myself. Cancer is hard. Of course it is. But life is hard too. It has ups and downs, but each time you push that comfort zone just a little bit, you will get closer to becoming the greatest version of yourself and everything else will become a little easier.

So, from here, give people your time, call up an old friend, write a hand-written letter to someone, do something different like a meditation class, smile more, the world is a reflection of yourself. Go find your challenge, whether it's physical, mental or social. And remember…

YOU GOT THIS!

Acknowledgements

Firstly, a thank you to the places where I wrote this book. The British Library, Dorchester Library, Weymouth Library and Bethnal Green Library. As well as my mum's shed. Libraries are so underrated. Great places!

Thank you to the people that proof read this book. Sometimes three times. If there's any spelling mistakes in here then it's your fault just as much as mine. Especially Lewis, Nas, John, Rhona, G Hanson, Ruth, Lois, Judith, Dan, and Louise.

Thank you to all of the medical staff that treated me during this journey. From Rio to Weymouth. You're all heroes! Thank you to everyone that works in healthcare to support patients. Thank you!

Thank you to my family for all the unwavering support and my two little dogs that brighten up my day.

Thank you to the people that always make me believe in myself. You know who you are. I appreciate every word.

Thank you to my writing coach Jacqui Lofthouse for coaching my storytelling techniques. Adding the sparkle on the top.

Thank you to the people in this book for letting me include you in the story. And to the people I didn't get to mention, I'm sorry but I love you equally as much. If not more.

Julian Quick

17th June 1988 – 5th February 2017

Somewhere over the rainbow. x

Support

Trekstock – For young adults with cancer
www.trekstock.com   @Trekstock

Macmillan Cancer Support
www.macmillan.org.uk   @MacmillanCancer

The Cancer Club – Lets get men talking
www.thecancerclub.co.uk   @The_Cancer_Club

Cancer Lads – Real men, real cancer stories
                @Cancerlads

Headspace – Mindset and Meditation
www.headspace.com   @Headspace

Fight To End Cancer – Global Cancer Fundraising
www.fighttoendcancer.com   @Fighttoendcancer

Af Marseh - Story-telling, motivation and public speaking
www.afmarseh.com   @AfMarseh

If you enjoyed this book please consider leaving a review
where you purchased it.
Thank you.